"I fell in love with this book. *We Have Always Been Here* is more than one person's memoir; it's a record of who and what we are as a people living in a time of great migrations, of cultures bumping into cultures, of politics of exclusions. In prose as economical, crisp, clear, and truthful as poetry, Samra Habib offers a map of how we might—each and every one of us—learn to see and treasure one another and ourselves. In this way it calls to mind the works of James Baldwin, Langston Hughes, and Jane Rule. I predict that this book will never go out of print— it will become required and desired reading for people of all ages, persuasions, and backgrounds. How I wish I had had it to keep close to my heart when I was younger."

SHANI MOOTOO, author of *Cereus Blooms at Night*

"Gutting and redemptive, *We Have Always Been Here* is the story of one woman's path to self-determination against every odd. Habib's voice is sensual and mesmerizing, her talent fierce and necessary. A transformative reading experience . . . Habib's every word lifts off the page, vital and bright as a match being struck."

CLAUDIA DEY, author of *Heartbreaker*

"A memoir of coming of age and coming out told in rich detail. Samra Habib's account of growing up queer and Muslim in

Pakistan and Canada is at once searching and tender. Weaving together the threads of her family history with her sexuality, faith, and culture, Habib speaks for a community that has often been muted, but writes with a voice and style that is all her own."

RACHEL GIESE, author of *Boys: What It Means to Become a Man*

"Samra Habib's memoir unfolds like a pre-digital photograph developing before our eyes. The identities she carries lovingly and with pride insist we revere a complication for so long denied. In the way that her photography and interview project, 'Just Me and Allah,' turned a tender gaze at queer Muslims each insisting 'I am here,' Habib's memoir demands 'See my selves.' To say I count, I exist, is revolutionary when you are denied complication. Habib has written the book she wished she had when she was young. It is a book we should all have had long ago."

MONA ELTAHAWY, author of *Headscarves and Hymens: Why the Middle East Needs a Sexual Revolution*

"Habib's graceful prose shines alongside the weight of her story and the fierceness of her message. A beautiful telling of a life, of love, of the reclamation of power, of feeling truly seen, and of finding your way home. An exquisite, powerful, and urgent book."

STACEY MAY FOWLES, author of *Infidelity* and editor of *Whatever Gets You Through: Twelve Survivors on Life after Sexual Assault*

We Have Always Been Here

A QUEER

MUSLIM MEMOIR

We Have Always Been Here

VIKING

Samra Habib

VIKING

an imprint of Penguin Canada, a division of Penguin Random House Canada Limited

Canada · USA · UK · Ireland · Australia · New Zealand · India · South Africa · China

First published 2019

www.penguinrandomhouse.ca

LIBRARY AND ARCHIVES CANADA CATALOGUING IN PUBLICATION

Habib, Samra, author
    We have always been here : a queer Muslim memoir / Samra Habib.

Issued in print and electronic formats.
ISBN 978-0-7352-3500-7 (softcover).—ISBN 978-0-7352-3501-4 (electronic)

1. Habib, Samra. 2. Muslim gays—Canada—Biography.
3. Lesbians—Canada—Biography. 4. Autobiographies. I. Title.

HQ75.4.H38A3 2019   306.76'63092   C2018-904290-7
                                                  C2018-904291-5

Cover and interior design by Jennifer Griffiths

Printed and bound in Canada

10 9 8 7

Penguin
Random House
VIKING CANADA

To chosen families everywhere

Even the most incorrigible maverick has to
be born somewhere. He may leave the group
that produced him—he may be forced to—
but nothing will efface his origins, the marks
of which he carries with him everywhere.

—JAMES BALDWIN

one

We both had shaved heads. Although the reason for mine was that a week earlier my barber had discovered head lice before giving me my monthly bowl cut, I suspect *her* reason was more exciting. I couldn't have been older than five when I saw her, but I can still vividly recall her face. My eyes fixed on it as honking trucks zipped by and three different qawwalis blared from the shops behind me. My mother likes to tell the story of how intently I would focus on the flickering television screen—the only one on our street in Lahore—while she nursed me. She would turn me around in an attempt to protect my eyes, but I always managed to swivel my head toward the screen. She would be the first to tell you: I've always been drawn to action.

My dad had parked the car in front of the shops in Liberty Market as my parents searched for last-minute Eid dresses for my sister and me. I always hated the muted colours my mother chose. Greys the colour of concrete or washed-out browns that reminded me of Ovaltine. As I waited in the back seat, I found myself drawn to the woman with the shaved head. Something about the spontaneity of her movements and the ease with which she rested her hand on her matte black motorcycle captivated me. She was probably closer in age to my mother, who was in her mid-twenties at the time, but the similarities ended there. I had never seen a woman laugh so freely in public and be so comfortable in her skin while socializing with men and women, as if that were a regular occurrence for women in Pakistan. Eventually she noticed my little face interrogating her from afar and smiled before shifting her attention back to a conversation with her friend. I seemed to be the only one fascinated by her: my younger sister continued to talk to herself—or maybe to me, who can say—in the back seat. Soon the woman was hiking up her black shalwar and adjusting her dupatta, securing it tightly so that her breasts were modestly covered—almost like donning armour before entering battle. She sped off on her motorcycle and joined the busy night-before-Eid traffic.

I'd only ever been surrounded by women who didn't have the blueprint for claiming their lives. There were my aunts, who would never be caught socializing without their husbands present—certainly not publicly. They couldn't drive their cars without their husbands, let alone ride a motor-cycle. And there was my mother, who was notified of her own name change only when her wedding invitations arrived from the printer. She stared at one for a few moments, wondering if my father had changed his mind and was marrying someone else instead. Without consulting her, he had decided that Yasmin would be a more suitable and elegant name for his wife than Frida. It was one of the first signs that her identity was disposable. Her free will was up for grabs, available to be stencilled over by my father and perhaps even by her children. Her role was to be a pious wife and an attentive mother. Being a sacrificial lamb meant a place would be reserved for her in heaven. Even if it meant that her life would be hell, surely Allah would see her sacrifice and allow her into *jannat*, the prized heaven.

I don't know much about my father's life before he met my mother, but I'd heard stories of him hitchhiking through Iran in the 1970s and working as a dishwasher in Hamburg for racist restaurant owners and coming close to death several times over the course of his travels. I'd look with curiosity at all the young Pakistani men in the black-and-white photographs from Istanbul, remnants of a life he's too ashamed to talk about. Years later he would insist that my brother keep his hair "short and respectful," yet in those early photos, which show traces of a life full of adventures, long, thick layers and wispy bangs frame his face as he looks back at the camera in a snug leather jacket and tight bell-bottoms, his hand resting on his waist. He would say that his life began when he married my mother, but I had to wonder whether he was simply trying to convince himself.

After a series of miscarriages, my mother became pregnant with me, at which point my great-grandmother—who had enjoyed the freedom of not having a husband for decades after being widowed—ordered my mother to move in with her. She was certain that the stress of being a dutiful wife and looking after my father and his family was not good for her pregnancy. For nine months, she and the older women in the family took care of my mother by making sure she was well fed, adequately rested, and had very little interaction with men. My father was to visit her only on Fridays until I was born.

When I was just six months old, my father embraced me tightly as he sped around on his candy-red Kawasaki, showing me off to his friends. I hadn't yet done anything to earn my parents' pride, but they were always so vocal about what a blessing I was. My mother still shows me pictures of the outfits she sewed and dressed me in solely so she could stare at me for hours. According to her, one of my first full sentences was "Stop staring at me."

"We prayed every day to have you," my father told me several times as he braided my hair before nursery school.

My mother would give birth to two more girls, each of us a year and a half apart. By the time their third daughter was born, family members and neighbours were in mourning. They would drop by unannounced and express their condolences to my parents for having yet another girl. Being parents to daughters meant mounting burdens; it didn't guarantee the prosperity that having sons did. Boys were free to go out and generate income for the family, whereas girls needed to be sheltered from the dangerous outside world until it was time to pass them on to their new guardians, their husbands. Daughters were additional mouths to feed, and dowries for them had to be accumulated before marriage. My father told the mourning guests to kindly go to hell, and in an act of stubbornness and, perhaps most important, love, named his third daughter Shazadi, meaning "princess."

Our growing family lived in a modest one-bedroom apartment in Angoori Bagh, a working-class neighbourhood of Lahore. Cats, goats, roosters, and children freely roamed the narrow, brick-lined streets. Mothers bathed their children outside with a bucket of water from a tap at the end of our street. Later in life, whenever I'd claim I was too good for something or that a garment looked cheap, my mother would gladly remind me that I used to piss barefoot outside in Angoori Bagh. Which was true. I would cover the bottom half of my body with a large shawl as I peed in the

5

drain beside our house, where dirty laundry water ran beneath me, smelling of the same laundry soap everyone in the neighbourhood used. We would get it from Naseem up the street, who was kind and trustworthy—unlike the men who would congregate at the foot of the hill that led to Naseem's convenience store. They hissed and murmured "*Bohat pyari gori hai*"—what a beautiful fair-skinned woman—at my mom as her grip around me and my toddler sister tightened and she raised her burka to ensure that only her dismissive eyes were visible. It seemed that no matter how much her burka covered her up and hid her silhouette, nothing could protect her from the vulgar comments and predatory eyes of neighbourhood men. Even being accompanied by her two young children wasn't enough to keep them at bay.

I liked going to Naseem's convenience store with my mom because I could pick out my favourite jam, usually strawberry, sometimes ginger-orange or apricot. It came with a miniature spoon as part of a giveaway. The spoons were too small to actually eat with, and I lined them up along the sill of the window that looked out into the alley. As soon as we got home from Naseem's store, I would make toast and slowly butter it right to the edges and then add a layer of my jam. I was always happy to find in my backpack the jam sandwiches my mom wrapped up in old newspaper, along with a thermos filled with Rooh Afza, a sugary rose-flavoured drink. Unlike the rotis and omelettes she packed for my lunch that remained untouched in the bottom of my bag, the butter and jam sandwiches were always devoured. Because it was a rare treat at the time, I felt cool in front of my friends as I ate my bread gooey with jam. My mother would tease me in front of guests for preferring instant, subpar foods to what she laboured over for hours at home.

When the small bedroom with two double beds and a cot felt too crowded, my dad laid out two charpoys in the veranda so my sister and I could fall asleep outside watching the stars while my parents slept inside with my baby sister. I enjoyed scaring my sister by mimicking a ghost we'd seen in a Bollywood blockbuster about a woman who'd come back to haunt her lover after twenty years. "*Bees saal baad*"—twenty years later—I'd chant in my best eerie voice. We woke up to roosters crowing and visits from wandering street cats, as women in adjoining houses prepared morning chai. The smell of cardamom, steaming milk, methane gas, and greasy sweet parathas perfumed the air. We lay wrapped in thin, much-laundered cotton sheets my mom had cross-stitched with flowers and leaves, cocooning ourselves from the heat of the morning sun. We worked on the puzzles in the morning newspaper until the sun's heat became too much for our tiny bodies to bear. When my mother finally needed us to get up, she yelled,

"Chai is ready." The announcement was the only alarm clock we needed.

After my father left for his sales job at an engineering company, I would watch my mother create patterns on her hand-knitting machine: boats, sheep, cars. She'd enrolled in knitting classes taught by an elderly widow, and when she started having problems producing milk for my baby sister, she sold her sweaters, hats, and tiny booties for neighbourhood infants so she could buy formula. Some days, my father's departure was my mother's cue to blast Bollywood songs on his tape recorder. He was the strict ruler of our household, and he'd made it clear to us—my mother included—that good Muslim women shouldn't dance or laugh or be heard. "Allah hates the loud laughter of women!" he'd bellow, raising his voice whenever we fooled around or were noisy. We were to reduce our joy to something faint or inaudible. So when he left, we would dance with her and let out our happier, joyful selves. There was an unspoken understanding that we could only be freely playful when he wasn't around.

And yet my father did occasionally show tenderness toward his daughters. I remember once informing him that I had volunteered to play a princess in the school play the next day and needed a crown. It was almost my bedtime and most of the shops were closed. Nevertheless, he set me on his motorcycle and I clung to him as he rushed to the market, now pitch-black and deserted. He parked his motorcycle in front of a grilled-corn stand and hoisted me onto his shoulders. We surveyed all the closed shops that were still lit to see if we could beg someone to let us make the last-minute purchase. Not only did we have to find someone who would open up their shop, but also we had to spot a place that sold a crown that fit a five-year-old aspiring thespian. We finally found a gift shop that sold copies of the Quran, prayer beads, and incense sticks. My father, sure that the shop would have just what we needed, tapped on the closed grille, trying to get the shop owner's attention. Perhaps softened by seeing a sleepy child perched atop this pleading man, the owner let us in. To my surprise, after a few minutes he emerged from the back of the shop with a small crown in his hands. Our faces lit up.

But my father couldn't pass up an opportunity to negotiate. "Ten rupees," he offered. The shop owner was insulted by the offer, and rewrapped the crown in the red silk dupatta and put it under a display of prayer caps. After ten minutes of bargaining with the exhausted man, we left the store with my new crown.

I always felt that my father was thrilled to have me as his daughter. No motorcycle trip was complete without my accompanying him. We would zigzag our way through the congested streets on our way to Anarkali Bazaar to get fresh lamb and haleem for dinner. I loved whiffing the aromas of cardamom, turmeric, simmering meat, and bubbling naan from the many cement ovens that erupted as large cylinders from the ground.

"What an angelic, selfless child," my mother used to say of how seamlessly I had transitioned to the role of older sister to two siblings—a toddler and a newborn who required the attention I'd once had all to myself. Perhaps she thought that if she repeated the statement often enough, it would eventually become true.

I remember feeling more guilt than pride at her insistence. I feared her disappointment when she would discover that I was actually incredibly jealous. It was the only secret I kept from my mother as a child, and the weight of it made me uneasy. I feared that the revelation would expose what a fraud I was, making me unworthy of my parents' love. I overcompensated by being extra nice to my younger sister when my parents were around. I made a big show of offering her pieces of my Choco Chum, a beloved Pakistani treat that consisted of button-like biscuits with dry milk chocolate inside. They always tasted as though the packages had been forgotten behind the cashier for years.

I was especially jealous of my cousin Ishma. Ishma and I were the same age, but she came from the wealthier side of my mother's family, made up of doctors, engineers, and professors who spoke fluent English. We saw them only a few times a year, when they came to visit or at our annual family picnics by a small stream close to Sadaar, where my great-grandmother lived. We usually went to Sadaar without my father, which meant my mother was more relaxed, free to laugh as loud as her heart desired. She would slice mangoes and pour salty lassi for everyone to drink, and I would wonder why only the boys and men in the family swam.

When these relatives came to visit Angoori Bagh, my resentment would flare up over Ishma's being allowed to stay up past our bedtime. As I tried to fall asleep, I could hear my extended family praising her drawn-out, nonsensical stories about Pathans who lived in mountains. "*Mashallah. Or! Or!*" they would cheer, begging for another tale. I thought, *What does Ishma know about Pathans in Peshawar while living in her giant house in a gated community in Karachi?* I was mad that I was never asked to share any of the stories I'd written, especially as my mother knew that I wrote them regularly. The only time I was invited to perform was when I was asked to tell everyone the name for what I was wearing, a long red and white polka-dotted nightie with short ruffled sleeves that I'd changed into before bed.

"A nineteen?" I would reply on cue, confused about what the big deal was. My mother had never corrected me. She and all my relatives would burst into laughter. I was humiliated, and I resented Ishma even more. But I never told my mother this, and I would be a model of neutrality whenever Ishma visited, even though I was secretly critical of her talents and envious of the enthusiastic reception everyone gave her, as if we were in the company of a Pulitzer Prize–winning writer.

When Ishma's father, a rich businessman, got her a starring role in an ad for Choco Chum, the whole family was alerted to when the commercial would debut, before and during *Tanhaiyan*. *Tanhaiyan* was a drama about two young sisters who, after their parents die, are forced to take up roles traditionally associated with men—a rare example of female empowerment on Pakistani television. They start their own business to support themselves and pay off the debt their parents left behind. For a brief moment my jealousy of Ishma was eclipsed by a new feeling: fear—that I would have to take care of my younger sisters if something ever happened to my parents. I imagined begging for money on the street with my baby sister in tow or selling jasmine necklaces to women in the passenger seats of cars during rush hour traffic, like many women and girls in Pakistan. I still associate the smell of jasmine in bloom with my mother, who would always buy a necklace for herself during family trips. The aroma of jasmine flowers would linger on her as I would lean in for a kiss long after the petals had browned and dried up.

Whatever reserve of jealousy I didn't spend on Ishma I directed at my friend Atika, who had moved to the neighbourhood with her family from Karachi. It was clear they were more well off than others on the street. Her family was building a house up the street while they temporarily lived in a smaller home closer to us. Instead of attending the one-room school my sister and I went to, just a few steps away from our house, Atika went to an expensive "English medium" school, where all the courses were taught in British English. She had short, shaggy hair and wore thick-framed glasses. I had never seen a kid my age wear glasses before. All of a sudden, I desperately wanted a pair for myself.

One day, after playing hopscotch on our street, we walked home together in the fading sunlight. My house was right before Atika's, and just as I was getting ready to say *Khuda Hafiz*—God be with you—she grabbed my hand and led me to her new house. It was still under construction, and everything was covered in dust—the entire house looked as though it had just been through an earthquake. I knew it wasn't safe for us to be there. When we reached the back of the house, Atika led me to the big reveal: two separate bathrooms, each equipped with a shower and toilet. I had never seen either in my entire life. After watching me play with the knobs, Atika let me shower. That glimpse into the world of luxury was intoxicating. We played until we heard Maghrib prayer on the mosque speakers, signalling that it was time to go home.

I didn't take it very well when Atika made a new friend. I saw it as a betrayal of our friendship contract. Rabia, the youngest of ten sisters, lived across the street. I remember throwing rocks at her as she played with Atika one afternoon. When I heard her scream, I hid behind a wall, then coolly walked back to my house and seated myself on the floor as my family set about eating dinner, not once feeling guilty about what I'd done. That's my last memory of Atika and probably the worst act I've ever committed out of jealousy.

If I were to write a play about my parents, I know precisely where the first act would end and the second would begin. One day my mother had some errands to run and no one to watch over me. My sister, then a rambunctious toddler, insisted on staying with her, so I was left alone under the care of a friend of my father's, someone my mother barely knew. I've chosen to forget his name and his face, but the damage he caused left an invisible scar that will last a lifetime. I remember a dark room, heavy curtains obscuring any hope of clarity. I felt his hands on my buttocks and inner thighs. At one point I noticed we were not alone—a woman I'd never seen before was watching from the edge of the bed. I'm not sure how long the incident lasted. It could have been minutes, or hours. I was four.

The next thing I remember is searching for my mother in the street and mistaking a woman in a similar burka for her. "Mama!" I cried. The woman turned around with a blank stare. I ran away in embarrassment as her laughter echoed loudly behind me.

When I finally found my mother and told her what had happened, she took me into the bathroom, her body trembling under the black fabric of her burka, her kajal-lined eyes displaying horror at the possibility of her worst fear being a reality. She examined me with the careful precision of a surgeon. Despite the sweltering heat, her touch felt cold and clinical. Once she determined that my hymen had not been broken, she uncovered her face by taking off her burka; finally, she could breathe as deeply as she needed to. She was too mortified to take me to the doctor, even though in the aftermath I couldn't stop coughing. My father was the only other person who could be trusted to know what had happened. She didn't dare discuss it with friends and family for fear of people speculating whether I was still a virgin, the worst possible outcome.

It became important to me to act as though I hadn't been scarred by the incident. I was so concerned with showing my mother that I'd survived the trauma unaffected that I actually believed I had. Instead of making her under-stand that it wasn't okay for her to leave me alone at that age with a man who was basically a stranger, I tried to make her believe I was okay, that she didn't have anything to worry about or any reason to blame herself. Even when I felt I was unravelling in front of her, I looked primped, pol-ished, and indestructible, because that's how she wanted to see me. She became an enthusiastic and adoring audience of my performance of put-togetherness, so I gave more of it. To this day, if I cough during a phone conversation with my mother, it provokes a flurry of inquiries.

"Why are you coughing?" she asks suspiciously.

"It's just a cold, Mom."

It would be far too easy to villainize my mother and her behaviour. But that is to assume she had the tools and the privilege to consider another future for her daughter. She was raised to believe that control was not something granted to women. Even with a tiny bit of control, there is always a caveat: you cover yourself up when conducting business with men; you get your husband's, brother's, or father's permission before you travel; and elders are always right, even when they aren't.

My mother's father, a globetrotting journalist, married my grandmother after falling in love with her ethereal beauty, without ever having a conversation with her. On their wedding night, he was disappointed to discover she had a stutter. Eventually he left her for someone educated and worldlier. In his mind, his new wife was his intellectual equal, something he thought my grandmother didn't have the capacity to be. My heartbroken grandmother was unequipped to take care of her six daughters and one son, and my mother, the eldest daughter, was often left to look after her siblings.

So my mother came of age knowing abandonment and neglect intimately. Her experiences taught her that as a woman, fertility, purity, and beauty were the only currencies she could exchange for a better life. She understood that any hindrance to my ability to find a suitable husband made me as undesirable and disposable as her stuttering mother. She lived in a country where countless women are found dead in alleyways and on the sides of dirt roads, their bodies discarded because they were not able to conceive children, particularly boys.

Before that day, I'd been free to play with my friends outside as long as I came home before Maghrib prayer. I would explore abandoned houses with my equally mischievous friends and terrify my archnemesis, Rabia, by screaming her name and hiding so she would think it was a jinni. But after that day, my parents did everything they could to ensure my sisters and I were never out of their sight, always accounted for. Sleepovers at our grandmother's were out of the question. Every activity was monitored and supervised.

I had lost my right to be a child. My parents hired a succession of nannies to watch over me at all times. Resentful that I could no longer do whatever I wanted, I would terrorize the nannies by refusing to do what they asked and, in extreme cases, becoming violent.

Uzma was the last nanny they hired before finally giving up. As we walked to the market one afternoon, we saw that a crowd had gathered at the foot of the street, preventing us from crossing the road. Uzma couldn't have been older than fourteen. Her long brown hair under her loosely fitted dupatta was lightened by the sun from her hours spent working outdoors, and her teal linen shalwar kameez was gently perfumed with jasmine oil. As we got closer to the growing crowd, her grip around my hand tightened. People cheered and applauded and we stopped walking, clueless about what was happening. All I could hear was a song from the Bollywood movie *Pakeezah*, a seventies cult favourite about a tawaif—a prostitute—named Sahibjaan whose mother is also a tawaif. In the film, Sahibjaan's fiancé, Salim, renames her Pakeezah, meaning "pure of heart," because that's how he wants to see her. Frustrated after being recognized by men who know her as a tawaif wherever she goes with Salim, she abandons him before their wedding, returning to the brothel where she believes she is destined to be. In one of the most significant moments in the movie, she sings and dances for a crowd that, unbeknownst to her, includes her biological father. Sahibjaan, in the song Uzma and I heard that afternoon, sings about people in the audience who are responsible for taking away her dupatta, implying her dignity, no matter how hard she tries to hold on to it. The odds are stacked against her.

As the crowd parted, my gaze met that of the hijra who had the entire audience of mostly men under her spell. She was dressed in a pink shalwar kameez similar to Sahibjaan's in her pivotal scene, and her long braid, woven through with golden threads, would periodically brush up against men, mimicking a forbidden flesh-to-flesh touch. She was aware of her limitations and how to subvert them. I was more captivated by her reimagining of Sahibjaan than by the actual Bollywood classic my father loved. Even at that age, I had a vague sense of the radicalness of a hijra—a person assigned male at birth who does not identify as male, but rather as "third-gender"—playing the role of one of the most desired female characters in Bollywood history and being the subject of male desire. Her hand gestures, pleading gaze, and gyrating hips alluded to her familiarity with the experience of an outcast woman wronged by those who were supposed to love and protect her. *I too have lost my dignity because of these people as a result of circumstances I have no control over*, her body language testified. I wanted to hear more.

Eager to get closer to the hijra and absorb every inch of detail, I stepped forward. Uzma yanked my hand, preventing me from joining the crowd of restless men. With all my strength, I pulled her hair, ripping a clump from her scalp. As she bellowed in agony, the music stopped and everyone, including the dancer, stopped to turn their attention to the source of the pained sound. I stood still, surrounded by the large crowd, with long strands of thick hair in my palm.

two

I woke up to the warm and peppery smell of pakoras frying in the kitchen. It was early for my mother to be making the oniony corn fritters—pakoras are usually served in the afternoon, with chai and thick cucumber raita, to tide one over before lunch or dinner. My mother hadn't yet woken us up for morning tea, which meant she wanted us to stay in bed as long as possible while she cooked in the kitchen. We were having company today for my birthday party. I was turning seven.

My mom was a sucker for birthday parties and weddings. Big celebrations gave her an opportunity to show off her dance skills, refined by mirroring the best: iconic Bollywood actresses like Zeenat Aman and Rekha, who often played on screen while she cooked or massaged our scalps with amla oil. They were also an excuse to be freely social. Women would come together on the rug-covered outdoor dance floors under hundreds of tiny twinkling lights, overjoyed that they could unabashedly be themselves. We would move to the rhythm of the dhol drum played at the henna ceremony, two thumps to the right and one to the left—*dhak dhak . . . dhak, dhak dhak . . . dhak*—and feast on lamb that had been roasting for days. This was before military ruler General Zia-ul-Haq's influence on the Islamization of Pakistan and we started seeing its impact in our everyday lives. He established Shariat courts to judge cases using Islamic law, and punishments like whipping, amputation, and being stoned to death were now common practice for criminal offences such as adultery and blasphemy. Religious minorities, like the one my family was a part of, were especially vulnerable to the courts' arbitrary rulings.

Our sect was founded in 1889 by Mirza Ghulam Ahmad, who wanted to reform Islam and remind Muslims of the beliefs laid out by the Prophet Muhammad. He emphasized non-violence and stressed tolerance of other faiths. Ahmadis believed Mirza Ghulam Ahmad's claim that he was the Promised Messiah, while other Muslims, mostly Sunni extremists, refused to accept the Ahmadiyya Movement and forbade us from calling ourselves Muslims. Ahmadis are regularly persecuted, legally and through extreme measures, for anything from using a traditional Muslim greeting in public to reciting the call to prayer. Stories of Ahmadi businesses being set ablaze and Ahmadi mosques being besieged by gunmen are sadly common. A cousin of mine narrowly avoided getting killed when Sunni extremists barged into a mosque during Friday prayer and opened fire. He managed to lead a group of attendees into the basement, but others weren't so lucky: attacks by grenades and rifles killed eighty and wounded ninety-five Ahmadi Muslims.

Ahmadis have a long history of being treated poorly, especially at the hands of the Pakistani government. In 1974, the Pakistan Peoples Party promised Ahmadis that if they supported the party, the bloc would work to end discrimination against the sect. My grandfather, father, and uncles worked tirelessly, campaigning and volunteering for the PPP in the hopes that they, along with millions of other Ahmadis, would be able to live freely. But when the party came to power in 1977, Ahmadis were declared "non-Muslim" after the new leader, Zulfikar Ali Bhutto, faced pressure from mullahs. This further escalated the violence and injustice the sect continues to face today.

When I finally got out of bed, I noticed that the yellowing walls of our kitchen and veranda were covered in small green decorative flags that matched the accent colour on our door frames and kitchen cabinets. The paint had started to peel, so we'd often find green chips on the floor and under the stove and stuck to our shoes. My father refused to add a fresh coat because that would signal his commitment to a place my mother desperately wanted to leave behind. He assured her that we would move to a bigger house as soon as our financial situation improved.

I felt a surge of happiness seeing the flags. The green of the Pakistani flag had come to symbolize winning: as students, we were awarded prizes wrapped in green tissue paper for coming in first in a badminton competition, and correctly singing the national anthem or getting a perfect grade on a dictation test earned a green star next to our name. For me, seeing green was like getting a pat on the back—something I rarely got at home.

Among the few invitees to my birthday party was Pinky, who lived upstairs and was more of an older sister to me than a friend. Pinky would come downstairs every day and keep my mom company while she cooked supper or washed clothes. She'd pitch in with chores, or fix my mom a pot of cardamom milk tea, letting me lick the skin of milk that would get stuck in the tea strainer along with cardamom seeds. The only other kid invited was Osman, who lived across the street. His family was Shia, and his mother was one of the few women to be let inside my mother's inner circle. Although Osman and I weren't close, he'd always make an effort to throw the ball to me when a group of us played football. We were in the same class, and he would often come over after school so that my mom could help us both with our homework.

I wished I could invite Sonia, whom I'd recently been forbidden to see. Sonia's mother, the neighbourhood tailor, sewed and embroidered beautiful garments that made all the local women feel like glamorous Bollywood stars. They'd each flaunt their signature styles at Friday prayer as though it were the Met Gala. My mother spent hours at the salon before going to mosque, getting her eyebrows threaded and her hair wrapped in rollers to give it just the right amount of bounce when her scarf fell to her shoulders during the sermon. She'd let the scarf rest there for a few seconds longer than necessary so that the aunties would notice the volume and colour of her hair and compliment her on it later. She would take pictures from *Stardust* magazine and yards of fabric to Sonia's mother and get stunning replicas back within days. Sewing clothes for the women in the neighbourhood was how Sonia's mom saved for her daughters' dowries—there were six of them, so she had her work cut out for her.

Sonia and I were the same age and instantly liked each other. She had a mischievous way about her that pulled me in. She always smelled of oranges, her fingers sticky from sucking on slices of the fruit as the juices dripped down her chin and hands. She left a trail of orange peels everywhere she went. I was in awe of her pin-straight hair that could do anything she wanted it to but mostly rested on her shoulders, two vertical lines framing her gamine face. Mine was curly and unruly, and my mother insisted on having it fashioned into an unflattering bowl cut. Since I was no longer allowed to go outside or visit friends without my parents chaperoning, much of our playing happened at our house. Sonia never asked why—I just let her believe it was because my parents were extremely religious. When we weren't building blanket forts, we spent afternoons on the veranda flashing everyone who walked by, spreading our legs wide open and exposing our vaginas, breaking out into peals of laughter with each look of horror we received.

Some days, Sonia wanted to play doctor. She'd pull down her pants and ask me to give her an injection, and I'd pretend to inject her warm skin with a piece of chalk, its tip pointy and startlingly cold. The chalky imprint of my hand would remain on her bum as she pulled up her pants, laughing. We'd often play in the musty, abandoned room on the second floor above our unit that was full of discarded furniture and yards of fabric my mother had purchased to bring to Sonia's mother. One day, when I suggested we tell each other stories instead of playing doctor, she began to tell me a dirty tale of two lovers, Idris and Sahar, who undressed in front of each other—but she abruptly ended the story just when my heart started racing with anticipation. I needed to know what happened next.

"I have to go," she blurted. "Next time!" She patted my mop of curls and grabbed her backpack, flashing me an impish smile on her way out the door.

For days, I waited for her to come back and finish the story. A week went by. Unable to bear the suspense any longer, I told my parents I was going to visit Sonia, knowing full well I wasn't allowed to venture out unaccompanied. When they prodded, I recounted the whole sordid story. As expected, my parents told Sonia's parents that she wasn't allowed to visit our house ever again.

It was nearing four o'clock and my mother still had to pick up a cake before the guests arrived and my dad came home from work. She asked Pinky to keep an eye on my sisters and me so that she could run some errands and swing by the bakery. She knew how much I loved the dense, spongy cake soaked in rosewater and layered with thick cream and ripe fruit. As she opened the door, the smell of burning tires infiltrated the hallway. Without giving it much thought, she headed out the door, the smell lingering in the air. After all, the birthday would be incomplete without the cake.

The bakery was only ten minutes away, so we were worried when an hour went by and neither my mother nor my father had come home. When my mother finally showed up, she had with her Osman and his mother, along with five other Shia families from the street. Sunni and Shia conflicts had erupted throughout Lahore, and my mother had gathered this band of strangers together and offered temporary refuge from the rioting in the streets. As Ahmadis, we were the only family in the neighbourhood to be spared the wrath of Sunni extremists. For once, the target wasn't us.

The cause of the conflict goes back some fourteen hundred years. Immediately following the death of Prophet Muhammad, the two sects clashed over who his successor should be. Shias believe that Ali, the Prophet's cousin and son-in-law, was the rightful successor, whereas Sunnis argue that it was Abu Bakr, the Prophet's trusted advisor. Centuries of bloodshed have followed. Shias claim that Sunnis have received preferential treatment from the Pakistani government since 1948, soon after Pakistan was founded, and that their freedom of speech is consistently threatened. Around the time of my birthday, things had gotten particularly violent after the assassination of Arif Hussain Hussaini, founding leader of Tehrik-e-Jafaria, a religious organization that represented the Shias.

Amid all the mayhem, I marvelled at how my mother had managed to find a cake when all the shops were either closed or vandalized. I was even more shocked that she had made it home safe, unaffected by the tear gas or the rioters who were setting fire to everything in sight, the thick fumes permeating our house through the roofless courtyard where everyone had gathered. To a seven-year-old, it seemed the world was coming to an end. If my mother was panicked that my father was still not home, she certainly didn't let it show.

I looked at Osman, who had taken refuge under his mother's arm and was pressing his nose against it. There were other children, too—some my age or younger, some old enough to require a burka to hide the curves of their bodies. I couldn't help feeling relieved that this time it wasn't us. But the fear I witnessed was intensely familiar. Who belonged if none of us did? I had never felt as close to Shias as I did that day.

My mother, perhaps opting for a distraction, removed the wrapping from the cake and placed it on the dining table. Pinky heated a pot of goat's milk for chai and poured it into eight terracotta cups. The smell of cardamom temporarily replaced the pungent odour of burning cars.

When the phone rang, my mother almost dropped the tray of pakoras and ran toward it. "*Kee haal hai?*"—How are you?—she asked ironically, knowing my father was probably plotting how to get home safely while police had blocked off access to our street. She spoke in Punjabi, the language my parents used when they didn't want us to know what they were talking about, not realizing we'd picked it up over the years.

We were startled by a flurry of loud knocks on the front door and the voices on the other side demanding that we open it. We all knew that the men outside were after the Shias hiding in our house. My mother hung up the phone and, with the help of the other women, pushed a heavy cupboard full of china and ceramics in front of the door. As the thumping persisted, she silently lit the candles on the cake, one for each of my seven years. Taking our cue from her calm demeanour, we all gathered around the table as if nothing out of the ordinary was happening. After a loud chorus of "Happy Birthday" drowned out the noise in the background, I blew out the candles. My mother carefully plated each dish with an equal slice of cake, pakoras, and chaat and handed them to everyone in our house.

Soon it was time for Maghrib prayer. Pinky and the other women lined the concrete floor with bedsheets, and we Ahmadis prayed with our Shia neighbours for the first time, our bodies so close there was barely space between us. My eyes wandered to the different placement of hands on the chests of our Shia guests, placed higher than I was accustomed to. It struck me that despite our differences, we were all terrified of the same people.

The knocks eventually stopped and we wondered if the riots had too. Then we heard a heavy thud on the roof. We all lifted our heads in panic, and mothers tightly clutched their children. Then my dad emerged from the top floor, climbing down the stairs to the courtyard. Eager to unite with us, he had scaled the wall of a house at the end of our street and jumped between the rooftops until he reached ours. I had never in my life been happier to see him.

———

Pinky was getting married in a few months to someone in America, a doctor. Her parents and her fiancé's parents sealed the arrangement after showing her pictures of Imtiaz. Pinky and Imtiaz had spoken once on the phone but had never met in person. At the time, I was desperate for an older sister, and Pinky filled that hole in my life. Her own younger sister, Ayesha, mostly kept to herself—I could barely get her to acknowledge my existence.

In the months leading up to Pinky's wedding, I stumbled across a letter from Ayesha in a newspaper column called "Three Women, Three Stories." Whenever my mother was too busy to keep an eye on me, I read the column's scandalous stories about affairs and forbidden romance. I usually flipped to the last page, which included confessions and pleas for advice from readers on matters that were troubling them—things they couldn't share with anyone else. Much was expressed in codes and ambiguous phrasings that I knew were referencing immoral acts I wasn't supposed to understand. The nature of the act was never explicitly stated, but the undercurrents of *gunah*—sin—were always present, intriguing me no end. The lesson of each story was crafted to keep women pious, the most common advice being to pray for forgiveness. The stories were meant to serve as cautionary tales for other women who might crave adventures outside their sheltered lives, but I was more interested in the titillating details of their romantic encounters—the stolen glances, the secret walks in the luscious Shalimar Bagh.

Ayesha's contribution was heartbreakingly honest: she was scared she'd be lonely once her sister, her closest friend, moved to the United States. The reply couldn't possibly have soothed her anxiety over the loss. It simply told her to get over it, as that is what happens to women—they move on to their new lives with their husbands. In the days following my discovery, I started to see Ayesha through sympathetic eyes. I desperately wanted to commiserate with her about Pinky's leaving, but I didn't want her to feel exposed. I just wanted her to know that I was sad too. I found it unfair that women were expected to leave everything behind once they married, as though their lives before that point had never existed.

I also wondered how my mother felt about Pinky's departure. She maintained a small, trusted inner circle, and Pinky was among the chosen few granted access. While the other women on our street showed up to one another's houses unannounced with trays of oranges and pine nuts and traded neighbourhood gossip, the women in my mother's circle didn't ask a lot of questions or require entertaining. They just showed up and left when my mother needed them to. She was too busy for frivolous interactions; she made every word count. They'd gather to talk while my dad was at work, and my mother would shoo me out of the room. I always wondered what they talked about and why I wasn't allowed to join. One showed up at our door once with a swollen eye. I knew that whatever they shared was too sacred for me to interrupt with my nosy presence.

At the time, my mother was a very suspicious person, convinced her enemies were casting spells on her. She'd take me with her to the *jadu wala*, a man who could reverse curses, contact spirits, and cleanse bad energies. He had ratty hair and wild eyes, perched on a stage before a devoted audience who'd come to him when all else had failed. Each guest would state a problem that needed fixing, and the *jadu wala* would close his eyes and spew gibberish until he made contact.

This was added fuel for my mother, who insisted she regularly saw ghosts. For her, these spirit encounters confirmed the existence of Allah. Her belief is that each of us has a *rooh*, a spirit, and when a *rooh* leaves the body, the person is dead. The world is full of *roohs* of those who've passed away. In my mother's telling, the visits all occurred at times when she was questioning her faith. *Roohs* would appear to her as matter-of-factly as the milkman who came by every afternoon to scoop milk into our *dechki*, a cast-iron pot, from his donkey cart. ("Don't make any wishes when the milk comes to a boil, or they won't come true," my mother would warn me as I watched the pot, waiting for it to steam. To a dreamer like me, the possibility was terrifying.) "Wa-Alaikum-Salaam," she'd reply to their greetings, as though to an old friend simply passing by. The *jadu wala* once told her an enemy had planted something behind her bed to put a curse on her. When we got home, she opened up the storage unit attached to her bed, and in the very bottom, tucked beneath children's storybooks and her gold jewellery, was a handkerchief covered in animal blood. We had no idea how it got there. The discovery was an occasion for her favourite slogan: "Allah will take care of it." It applied to countless scenarios, and she would say it without missing a beat, with the assuredness of someone who has literally seen it happen. She would often say to me, an impatient child always looking for a clear answer, "*Jab hona hoga, ho jayega*"—whatever is meant to happen will happen.

Perhaps, then, she was the least surprised when our luck actually did change. My father had started buying land in up-and-coming neighbourhoods in Lahore, building houses and then selling them for much more than he'd invested. We were no longer living in one-bedroom flats in poor neighbourhoods, five of us on two large beds. At our new house, there was room for six—having given birth to three girls, my mother had her first and only boy, Bilal. Our new neighbours were upper middle class, with children who would list off all the countries they'd travelled to. Italy, Japan, England, and America were places I couldn't even find on a map yet. New shopping plazas were opening up nearby, with restaurants, bookshops, video stores, and clothing boutiques. I loved picking up English books, which I'd never owned before.

I'd watch my father intently as he worked on floor plans for new homes, familiarizing myself with the drawings for staircases, bathrooms, kitchens, and bedrooms. It was especially exciting to see the plans come to fruition. Soon enough I was sketching my own floor plans. The house I drew over and over again was patterned on the row houses in the opening sequence of *Full House*, one of the only American shows that aired in Pakistan. I'd design an entire top floor just for me—a place to write my stories in peace—making sure there was a glass wall so that my family could keep an eye on me.

I marvelled at the houses my father built: wide open rooftops built to enjoy the sky from the comfort of home, elegant columns from floor to ceiling. The smell of fresh paint and sawdust thrilled me. My dad would share his floor plans and architectural drawings with me and ask for my input—I felt I had a role to play in planning the layout of the houses we eventually lived in. I argued with my father on many occasions about the style of columns and gates he should choose, pointing out ones I liked when we were driving around on his motorcycle. I wanted a house that would make me feel safe and comfortable.

My mother had enrolled us in a military school because it was one of the best ways to ensure that my sisters and I got a decent education. Finally, I was attending an "English medium," just like my cousin Ishma. Non-Ahmadi military wives my mom had befriended in our new neighbourhood vouched for us and kept our being Ahmadi a secret. My mother had charmed them by being their confidante and bringing them gifts from Liberty Market.

Now it was more important than ever not to share any details about my life. Hiding that I was Ahmadi, as my parents had taught me to do, became part of my everyday reality. Changing schools wasn't the only catalyst for our training sessions; my parents seized any opportunity—while dressing us in the morning, during meals around the dinner table—to instill in us the importance of concealing this facet of our identity. Stories of relatives who'd been violently harmed for being Ahmadi were all the warning I needed. On long family road trips, my parents often complimented me because I had learned to remain silent, while my sisters loudly named every animal they saw grazing on the farms we drove past. "Be like Samra, stay quiet," they would demand. I learned to see being quiet as a virtue.

In my first year of military school I met Khola, a cool and rambunctious kid with the fluffiest of curls that would reveal tiny flecks of gold in the afternoon sunlight. Her eyes were the same shade of hazel as those of my cousin Ishma and her siblings—I knew it well from the annual family portraits sent to us from Balochistan: a brood of hauntingly gorgeous children in red embroidered tribal clothing and elaborate jewellery. Each year, the photograph would feature a new addition to the family, until there were too many children to orchestrate a photo shoot. Instead we got updates about individuals. One of the daughters got married off, *Mashallah*. The eldest son just bought his own rickshaw, *Subhan Allah*.

For most of that first year I admired Khola from afar, imagining what her home life was like. My classmates were just as drawn to her as I was. She had a natural coolness about her that I've searched for in others ever since.

One afternoon, as I made my way through the crowd at the Ahmadi mosque during Friday sermon, I noticed a girl with dark auburn curls peeking out from a tightly wrapped white dupatta. My heart stopped: it was Khola. She must have felt my gaze on her, because she turned around and smiled. She made her way toward me and we hugged and shared our surprise at seeing each other at the mosque. Soon the *adhan* came on, signalling that the prayer was about to start, and I returned to my mom's side. I felt relieved and energized by the discovery that I wasn't alone in this secret: someone I saw every day at school had to hide who she was as well.

The next day in class, I eagerly greeted Khola and told her how nice it was to see her at the mosque. "What are you talking about?" she replied. "That wasn't me."

By the late 1980s, things had grown even more unsettling for Ahmadis. My dad's older brother had no choice but to relocate to Rabwah, Pakistan, with his pregnant wife and children. In his family's last days in Lahore, imams instructed shop owners not to sell him any food, and they obliged, afraid their businesses would be shut down. My dad's cousin had been beaten up on the street by Sunni extremists, simply for being an Ahmadi. He knew that there was no point going to the police; they often stood back and watched such violations. When my father took longer than expected to return from a meeting to buy some land, I was terrified that he'd been conned into meeting with extremists who would kill him. I would cry in a panic until he returned home safely.

The Ahmadiyya community had moved its headquarters from Qadian, in India, to Rabwah shortly after Pakistan was founded in 1947. The city is home to many graves of Ahmadis, including my grandparents, who were gone before I was born. Visiting their tombstones was one of the many reasons we made the trip out there every year—it's the only connection I ever had with them.

Crossing the Chenab River to Rabwah with my family every year symbolized our brief foray into freedom. It meant that the people we walked by on the streets were, in a way, family. They were just like us, fearful of repercussions from mullahs beyond Rabwah. I remember seeing graffiti on a wall in Rabwah that read WHOLESOME SECURITY OF ISLAM AND THE FAITH LIES IN TOTAL LIQUIDATION OF AHMADIS: a reminder that although we were in the company of other Ahmadis, we were never immune from cruelty.

There were friends I saw each year in Rabwah, like Alia, who always complimented me on how soft my hands were when we played patty cake, shouting *"Rooey! Rooey!"*—the Urdu word for cotton. The last time we saw each other, before my family left Pakistan, we had spent the entire day together, and she told me to close my eyes while we were changing for dinner. We'd changed in front of each other many times before and not once had she told me to close my eyes. I covered my face with my hands, allowing a tiny gap between my fingers. Alia lifted up her linen kameez, and there they were: tiny breasts that hadn't been there a year ago.

My memories of Rabwah are also of the mountains, the open sky, and the streets lined with trees so tall I would cramp my neck trying to see their tops. The air smelled like pine, mud stoves, and henna waiting to dry. Because there weren't any tall buildings to obstruct the views, everything felt open. The sky was always crystal blue. The kind of freedom I experienced in Rabwah during family visits was unlike anything I experienced back home in Lahore. At night, when it got cold, I cozied up to my cousins in the crowded bedroom all the women shared. I was soothed by the smell of the jasmine oil we had massaged into one another's hair. The women in the family fetched water in a bucket from the tap outside the house and took turns bathing all the children who lined up. There was always a big dinner party to attend, often hosted by my uncle. He would order lamb nihari and chicken karahi from a nearby guest house. At night the stars were so bright they lit our hair and skin, sun-kissed from playing outside all day without fear. One cousin would examine my palm and tell me what a long life I was going to live and how much I was going to travel. My parents felt that we were safer in Rabwah, so I was allowed to roam the streets with my cousins and friends, often spending hours at the library, where I learned my grandfather had once worked. People in that city knew my ancestry better than I did—it was as though all Rabwah's citizens had grown up in the same home. Rabwah was the closest I ever came to being in the company of people I shared a history with.

Despite the relief Rabwah offered, my dad couldn't move his business there—Rabwah is a modest place with simple houses that have the bare necessities, and the houses my dad built were for affluent people. In 1990, disillusioned by continuing attacks on Ahmadi mosques and by government-sponsored discrimination toward Ahmadis, he started making arrangements for us to leave the country. President General Zia-ul-Haq's 1985 statement had provided an incentive for him to get out: "We will, Inshallah, persevere in our efforts to ensure that the cancer of Qadianism"—Ahmadis—"is exterminated."

Canada sounded like an appealing place to resettle because of its reputation for welcoming people like us. Even though we didn't know when we would get our passports, my dad started preparing by selling our house; we moved into a small flat. Everything felt temporary. I didn't see any point in studying for my exams or learning to cross-stitch in sewing classes, since we might leave at any moment. Investing in friends seemed futile. "My family is leaving for Canada," I warned the new crop of students at the beginning of the school year, just so no one would get too close.

The truth was, despite the possibility that my father could be killed or taken to jail if we stayed, I didn't want to leave. I loved Pakistan. It was all I knew. I loved my family, my cousins, my grandmother. The smells of the country still haunt me to this day—I seek them out in other places and people. It felt terribly unfair that we had to leave behind all that we knew, and I sulked openly whenever my parents discussed our plans.

One night, my mother came into the bedroom I shared with my sisters and woke us up. She'd received a phone call from the travel agent: we had only a few hours to leave the country. My dad would stay behind to take care of some business and follow us in a month. Half-asleep, I put my pink Velcro sneakers on the wrong feet and strapped on my backpack, double-checking to make sure it contained the new Barbie I'd already outfitted with a fresh pixie cut. As my father drove us to the airport, I thought about how much I would miss Pakistan. I wanted to throw a tantrum, but instead I just did what I always did on family car trips: I stayed quiet.

three

"So, how does it feel?" asked the immigration officer, a middle-aged redhead with a smattering of freckles.

Her question wasn't directed at anyone in particular—she repeated it a couple of times, eager for one of us to respond. I hoped my silence would imply that I didn't understand English. I was too busy studying her lurid red hair and her pale skin, as though she were an exotic creature. I'd never seen hair that wasn't as dark as my own up close before.

"So, how does it feel?"

I racked my brain for an answer that wouldn't complicate our chances of staying. I wasn't used to anyone asking me how I felt, and her question made me pause and wonder why. Why hadn't my parents ever asked me how it felt to leave behind people I loved? Why hadn't they asked me how I felt about my mandatory Princess Di haircut? In my world, you weren't asked how things *felt*. Parents and elders made your decisions for you. I'd never imagined there was an alternative, that I would ever have the opportunity to make a case for what I actually wanted.

"Good, thank you," I finally replied, playing the role of obedient refugee. Really, I was silently thanking her for not putting us in handcuffs. Upon our arrival at Immigration at the Toronto airport, I'd watched in horror as a group of asylum seekers were cuffed and escorted away. Tired and anxious after our thirty-hour flight, with stopovers in Frankfurt and London, I was terrified thinking what might happen to them. Would we meet a similar fate? What made our story more convincing than theirs? And what would happen to them once they were returned to the country they had escaped? My mother, with three young daughters holding on to her, a toddler son in her arm, and a young man beside her—my first cousin Nasir, who'd made the journey over with us for reasons that were still unclear to me—was given a lucky break. I didn't want to seem ungrateful by telling the immigration officer how I truly felt.

Being the most fluent English speaker in the family, I quickly shifted into the role of parent by translating for my mother. I felt it was my job to put her at ease, to help her make sense of this new reality that I hadn't yet come to terms with myself.

After a few hours of questions and filling out forms and waiting, we were finally permitted to leave the confines of the airport. In anticipation of what lay beyond the sliding glass doors, I thought back to the lush green landscapes I'd seen in episodes of *Little House on the Prairie*. That is what I imagined Canada—the entire Western world, for that matter—would look like. Miles of green hills dominating the horizon. Rich with abundance. Nothing like Pakistan. In my ten-year-old mind, war and persecution didn't exist this many oceans away from home. Bodies weren't disposable.

But that is not the Canada I encountered on that ripe July day in 1991. Instead of blooming with potential, Canada felt oddly sterile. Or maybe overly polite, as though it didn't want to ruffle any feathers with a jolt of personality.

We waited for our ride alongside other refugee families— aunts, grandparents, mothers, fathers, and cousins who looked like my own, with suitcase tags narrating their journeys from turmoil to relative safety: Lahore International Airport, Somali Airlines, Grozny Airport, Air Lanka. Their eyes lit up hopefully every time a new vehicle pulled in.

Restless, I decided to toy around with everything at the airport that looked foreign to me while my mother kept telling me not to go out of her sight. After making a pretend call from the phone booth, I found myself transfixed by the vending machine, stocked with brightly coloured candies and cans of pop. I spotted the button for Coca-Cola, the only familiar sight during those first few hours in the country, and begged my mom to give me some change from the embroidered satin purse that housed all our passports. I wanted to know if Coke tasted the same as it did back home, keen to find some thread of continuity. It took a while to sort through what little currency she'd managed to exchange in Pakistan, and then to distinguish a quarter from a dollar. I was surprised to see a chilled can tumble out instead of the glass bottle I was familiar with. (Back home, jewellery store owners would offer us bottles of Coca-Cola and Fanta while my mother tried on gold necklaces, earrings, and bangles for Eid and other big family gatherings.) I opened it and took my first gulp, and was shocked by the concentrated flavour and intense fizz. I realized that what we'd been drinking back in Pakistan was a watered-down version—already it felt like a distant memory. My sisters and my mother insisted that I let them take sips from my can, as if eager to experience the first cold and unnaturally sweet taste of the Western world.

Eventually we were picked up by a family friend, a man in his sixties who'd emigrated from Pakistan a few years earlier and was now embedded in a new mosque community in Canada. We'd be staying with my aunt, my father's sister, who'd made the trek here a year earlier with her three children, two sons and one daughter, all older than me. We hadn't been very close in Pakistan, but now we had no choice—we were bound together as outsiders in a new country.

When we arrived at my aunt's apartment, my cousin who was closest in age refused to speak to me in Urdu, even though he'd only been in Canada a year. It was as if he were using his fluency as proof of his superiority over me.

"How long does it take to speak perfect English?" I asked him.

"Six months," he replied without missing a beat.

I wondered how long it would take me to forget the language I dreamt in, stripping the proof of otherness from my speech.

My aunt's apartment building was one of two high-rises that housed a high concentration of Ahmadi families. These buildings were a sort of incubator for new immigrants: a place where they could save money and learn English so that they could eventually flee to the suburbs, leaving their apartments for the next wave of refugees trying to escape persecution. The one- and two-bedroom suites were often crowded with extended families, and ours was no exception—my two sisters and I shared a bed, and Nasir slept on a mattress in the area where a dining room table would normally go. Since we all slept close to the kitchen, the smells of cardamom, tamarind, and garlic powder permeated everyone's hair and bedsheets.

It was a strange neighbourhood for Ahmadis to flock to: there weren't any Pakistani businesses nearby, and for the most part we lived in a bubble, barely associating with people who were not Pakistani. There was a strip mall nearby with a department store, a dollar store, and a supermarket that didn't sell basmati rice, so my mother made biryani with risotto rice. (She also used MSG as salt, confused by the packaging.)

Throughout the day the building's parking lot would be filled with taxicabs, which the men drove to support their families, often sharing duties among themselves. One would sleep during the day after chauffeuring drunk clubgoers around all night, periodically cleaning up vomit in the back seat, and the other—the son or father or uncle— would drive people to business meetings and important lunches. I'd heard tales from the men in our extended family and community: how passengers would ask them where they were from with feigned curiosity, oblivious to the existence of their hometowns in Punjab, Sindh, or Balochistan. How they professed to love Bollywood and butter chicken, not realizing that those came from a different country altogether. They didn't even notice that the person driving the cab wasn't the same person on the taxi's registration staring right at them behind the driver's seat.

The basements of these buildings often doubled as makeshift mosques and gathering spaces for women. Although we were connected by the thread of discrimination that had made us leave our homes to build new ones, I had little in common with the other girls my age who looked and smelled so much like me. Sure, whiffs of turmeric also erupted from their delicately draped dupattas and thick, silky hair, but their days were spent whispering about their crushes on the Ahmadi boys who played cricket in the communal park between our two buildings. They plotted various ways to get their attention, hungry for a smile, a wink, even a glance. I couldn't connect with their secret plans to "accidentally" bump into their crushes or any other grand flirting schemes. They had no use for me. If I did end up playing with other girls at the park, it was with the ones who looked different from me, with names full of consonants that teased my tongue in delightfully unfamiliar ways: *Fabiola, Renata, Emeline, Giselle*. I shared the seesaw with Portuguese girls, admiring their intricate braids secured by tiny pastel-coloured barrettes. I chased Haitian girls down the slide while the aunties looked on with suspicion.

But often I spent time in the park alone, lingering among the rose bushes. The smell reminded me of lying in our lush garden back home, where I would water the roses during the hot summer months and think to myself, *This is where I would like to die.* Maybe that was a morbid thought for a kid my age, but not so surprising for someone who so deeply craved permanency—after all, what was more permanent than death? I would inhale the sweet, heady scent of the roses and touch their silky petals, and for a brief moment Canada felt familiar—like home. I could take refuge in the pistil, the anther, and the rosebuds, because there was continuity in those details. Roses I could be sure of.

One day, after hearing my mom complain about how fast the money she'd brought with her was disappearing, I went to the edge of the park lined with rose bushes. I began to gather them together into small bunches and fasten them with blades of grass. Each bouquet had two white roses with one that was glisteningly red. I surveyed the park for willing customers: teenagers shyly flirting on dates, old couples on park benches licking identical vanilla ice cream cones dotted with sprinkles, dads pushing their children on the swings. I made sure that none of the men I approached knew my family or looked as though they could be from the mosque. I knew that a young girl from the community approaching men would be cause for alarm and that I would hear about it from my mother. That afternoon, I managed to sell ten bouquets for two dollars apiece. I loaded the pockets of my yellow cotton shorts with my earnings, the weight of the coins causing them to slide down my bony, boyish frame. (Despite my best efforts, I had failed to put on weight; every evening, just before the sunset glazed our apartment with an orange glow, I'd sit at the dinner table with a tub of butter and a bag of white bread, eating every buttery crumb in the hopes of developing the kind of curves that fought their way out of my mom's kurta, which she wore only at home, where concealing her shape was not a priority.)

Back in our apartment, I triumphantly spread the change across the coffee table, one of the only pieces of furniture we owned, aside from a floral couch someone from the mosque had given us. My mother stared at the pennies, quarters, and loonies, speechless. I could tell she was angry, but I didn't understand why. I'd watched her put a tube of lipstick back on the shelf after mentally converting rupees to Canadian dollars. I'd heard her fret about money and whether we'd have enough for next week's groceries. It had been a drastic shift—only a few months ago we had a personal cook to prepare my mother's favourite dishes and I was attending one of the best schools in Lahore—so I was especially attuned to these new anxieties.

"Samra, that's not how you can help me. I don't need money from you," she said in a stern voice as I stared at the sun spots that had emerged on her hollowed cheekbones. "It's not safe for you to go around selling things to strangers. Never do that again."

I left the coins on the table, just in case she changed her mind.

I wanted to scream "I'm going back to Pakistan!" or cry out for my dad as my toddler brother had taken to doing, but I held my tongue. I didn't want to sound ungrateful;

I knew how difficult it had been to arrange this move. But to me it seemed we'd simply traded one set of anxieties for another. Sure, we were no longer afraid of being killed by religious extremists on our way to school, but not knowing whether we'd be able to make next month's rent didn't ease my mind either. We had our asylum and our government-issued blankets, but I still didn't feel free to be a child.

My father finally arrived in Canada on August 14, the day of Pakistan's independence, the height of summer—and the day I got my first period. After noticing blood in the toilet and watching it run down my legs, I cried out for my mother, convinced I was dying. She came into the bathroom, looked at my legs, and matter-of-factly announced that I was now a woman. This news surprised me—I felt I needed more time, I wasn't ready yet. My body still looked nothing like hers, and the things I'd learned while translating at her gynecologist appointments had mortified me.

When I came out of the bathroom, hoping for clarification on what was required of me in this new role, she had only one piece of advice: "Samra, stay away from boys. They only want one thing. They are not to be trusted." I tried to extract meaning from her words. My mother has a habit of answering straightforward questions with vague Urdu poetry, codes that needed to be deciphered. As a result, I'd been trained to look for meaning in unlikely places, in things unsaid. But this time I was stumped. All I knew was that my body was sore, and that didn't have anything to do with boys. Besides, boys weren't even on my radar. It was impossible to imagine what they might want from me, or what I might want from them.

After an awkward tutorial on maxi pads, we headed to the airport to welcome my father to Canada. As I waited for him to walk through the arrivals gate, I thought of all the times I'd feared losing him back in Pakistan. There were family trips through Punjab by train, when he would run out to get chai and pine nuts during stops and I'd scream after him, "*No, Papa!*" I'd keep my eyes glued to the window, and each time the train rattled as new passengers boarded I'd worry that we were going to leave the station without him. My mother would tighten her grip around my waist, cooing softly into my ears that Papa would come back to us in no time. On one occasion, the train actually did start to move before he returned. Hot tears trickled down my cheeks as I called out for him. Suddenly he emerged from the narrow train hallway, almost knocking over the new passengers scrambling to find seats, holding hot cups of tea and pine nuts rolled up in newspaper, smiling triumphantly as though he'd tempted fate and won.

But when we finally saw him that day, it was clear that a shift had taken place, as though a different version of him had walked off the plane. This new version moved through the world with doubt and uncertainty. He looked startled when approached by unfamiliar people, and he lacked authority in a way I had never witnessed before. Where was the man who used to drive me around on his motorcycle, expertly manoeuvring his way through the narrow, labyrinthine streets of Lahore? For the first time, I had become familiar with a place before he had.

My father's shame would especially flare up during our appointments at the welfare office, when my translating services were again required. Before every appointment, I would watch my mother anxiously smooth out the wrinkles in her burka and go to the bathroom several times. We could all hear her throwing up, even with the tap running and the toilet flushing. My parents who owned luxurious houses in Pakistan now had to convince a welfare officer devoid of emotions and sympathy that they needed money to survive and to pay the next month's rent, that it was necessary to get additional welfare help so that we wouldn't have to move to a shelter. My father refused to take the kinds of jobs available to someone who didn't speak much English— dishwasher, taxi driver, hotel cleaner—and I resented him for it whenever the possibility of having to move to a shelter with strangers loomed. I didn't understand why he couldn't step up and protect us at all costs. Instead he sat on the couch and watched TV all day, slowly fading into a distant version of his former self. Why had he given up on himself? Why had he given up on us?

September was upon us soon enough, and with it the day I was dreading: I was starting grade six at a brand-new school where I didn't know a soul. I walked the long hallway, lined with lockers and filled with kids chattering excitedly with one another, as though I'd been transported to a different planet. I wasn't used to seeing boys and girls mingling freely in public. With my short hair and the grey cotton dress trousers my dad had picked out at Goodwill, I wasn't exactly putting my best foot forward—surely no one wanted to befriend the awkward, androgynous new kid from Pakistan. While we waited in line outside our classroom, I scoped out what the other kids were wearing: dresses paired with combat boots, baggy pullovers with images of people I didn't recognize, and oversized jeans that barely stayed on. I could feel them staring back at me, sensing my nervousness. One even blurted out, "You're wearing boys' pants!" as though it were the worst thing in the world. My new classmates broke out laughing. The door finally opened, and a large man with skin as dark as my father's emerged to greet us. When he left the classroom for a moment and returned with a handful of chalk, I stood up from my seat, a sign of respect I was taught in Pakistan—and yet another reason for my classmates to laugh at me.

"Hush!" the teacher barked. The room went silent immediately. "Samra," he said, looking up from the attendance sheet. "Are you new to Canada?"

I nodded.

"I'm Mr. Daniel," he said. "*Aapka kya haal hai?*"—How are you?

My jaw dropped. I'd never met someone who could speak Urdu and didn't have a Muslim-sounding name.

"*Aap Pakistan sai hai?*" I asked him if he was from Pakistan as well. He wasn't. He was a Catholic born in India.

"Does that mean you're a Paki?" a redhead with Shirley Temple curls sitting beside me inquired. I didn't know how to respond, so I just flashed a clueless smile. I hadn't yet realized the harmful impact of that slur. Judging from the chorus of kids' laughter, I could only tell that being called Paki was not a compliment.

I started an ESL class shortly after. The class was full of new immigrants who were also confused by the insults and racial slurs hurled at them each day. Our teacher, Ms. Nakamura, was a kind Japanese-Canadian woman who was extremely excited about her job. Every word we

pronounced and enunciated correctly was a personal victory for her. On the first day, she spread a map of the world
on the floor and asked us all to indicate where we were
from, marking her own initials, T.N., next to Tokyo. Her
descriptions of the serene landscapes in Japan made me
want to see them myself one day. One by one, we marked
our initials on the map—on Bangladesh, Vietnam, Jordan,
Nepal, Afghanistan, China, and Cambodia—saturating
Asia with letters until there was no space left. I marvelled
at how we could all be from the same continent and yet
have taken such different journeys to get to this classroom
in Toronto. The best thing about being taken out of my
regular class—besides the temporary relief from being
bullied—was the field trips we took to familiarize us with
the city we now called home. We would go to the art gallery
or venture out to High Park and watch morning joggers run
by the ravine. Once, during the holidays, we went to a big
shopping mall downtown.

But outside of ESL class the humiliations abounded,
whether I was teased for being Paki, as the girls in gym
class liked to remind me, or for looking so malnourished
and skinny, or for using the British English I'd picked up in
Pakistan.

Lisa, Tara, and Angie were the worst offenders. I'd
learned how to deal with most of the others: stay out of
their way so they forgot that I existed; never raise my

hand, even when I was dying to share the answer to a math problem, for fear of being made fun of for my accent; feign illness in gym class to avoid having balls thrown at my face or being shamed for my body odour, a result of the spices in my mom's cooking that clung tenaciously to my skin and clothes. (I would spend years amassing an impressive collection of perfumes and body oils, as if no amount was enough to mask the stench of my shame.) The rotis my mother prepared for me and wrapped in newsprint were sometimes casually spat on. Several times a week I'd scrounge together enough change to indulge in pepperoni pizza and chocolate milk, learning only later from a kid who went to my mosque that pepperoni was *haram*, or forbidden.

Three months in, Ms. Nakamura declared that I no longer needed ESL. My English was strong, and I was perfectly equipped to attend regular classes. She assumed that such an evaluation would be a badge of honour for a new refugee kid dying to be accepted, but what she didn't realize was that ESL class was my safe haven. I was terrified of the wickedness that awaited me outside its doors. There was no predicting what might set off girls like Lisa, Tara, and Angie.

I learned the hard way in music class. Each student had to choose the instrument he or she would spend the year learning to play. Afraid that if I leapt up to claim a popular instrument like the clarinet or the flute I would be punished for it later, I waited for my classmates to choose before me. At last I inherited my fate—the trumpet. I wasn't looking forward to signing out and dragging the big, heavy case home to practise, but part of me wanted to surprise my teacher with a perfect rendition of "London Bridge Is Falling Down." Teachers, I was starting to learn, were my biggest champions. They rooted for me, and I dreaded letting them down. The bullies started being cruel to me only when the teachers looked away, so all I had to do was keep their eyes on me, the immigrant kid exceeding expectations. Energized by my plan, I rushed to the music room after school to claim my trumpet. As I dragged the cumbersome case out of the room, I glimpsed Angie out of the corner of my eye. Knowing that she also played the trumpet, I walked away as fast as I could.

The next day, a mousy girl from my class told me someone had an important question to ask me in the stairwell. Even though deep down I knew this couldn't be good, I obediently followed her instructions. Under the staircase, hidden from the herds of students making their way to class, were Lisa, Tara, and Angie. Angie glared at me with her icy blue eyes. I stood paralyzed, a lone car on the road about to collide head-on with a truck. Without saying a word, she slapped me on the cheek. The heat from the impact coursed through my body as the three girls broke into laughter. I fled to a bathroom stall to cry in private.

When I got home from school that day, before I could even consider telling my parents what had happened, my mom asked me if I could help her with her ESL homework— she was enrolled in a mandatory class so that we could collect our welfare cheques. I sat down beside her on our hand-me-down couch, took out a pencil, and showed her how to use an adjective in a sentence.

four

I was enjoying an episode of *Full House* after school one day when I felt Nasir's eyes on me, which I often did, particularly when no one else was around. But that day, his gaze had purpose and intention. I had just changed out of my oversized sweatshirt and baggy jeans—necessary to fit in at school—and into the linen shalwar kameez my parents insisted we wear at home. *Full House*, like the scar on my cheek that remains from childhood chicken pox, was one of the few constants from my life in Lahore, as it was one of the only American television shows to meet Pakistan's strict religious criteria. I was watching with rapt attention when Nasir got up, handed me a note, and immediately retreated to his bedroom.

Nasir had been living with us since we moved to Canada. He worked as an assistant manager at 7-Eleven, and his contribution to the rent was welcome, considering our financial situation. He would keep some of what he earned to pay for essentials—bus passes and tickets to

Bollywood movies at the theatre in Little India—and send the rest back home to Pakistan to help out his parents and younger siblings.

Somi,

I'm not supposed to give you this letter. Your mom will be very upset if she know. I'll be in big time trouble. Please don't tell anyone. She told me to keep secret until you turn 18. She said 13 is too young for you to know about this situation. You and I supposed to be married. I'm your fiancé. We get married when you turn 18. Your mom made arrangement.

Nasir

It was clear he'd ripped a page out of my Hilroy notebook to relay the news that despite having grand dreams of becoming a writer and travelling the world, my future consisted of being a good Pakistani wife. I was destined for a life of servitude, just like Nasir's mother, my mother, and my mother's mother, who all muted their ambitions and defining traits to be pious *sisters*, getting lost in a sea of burka-clad wives.

To distract myself from the weight of the note's message, I studied its superficial details. Although Nasir was ten years older than me, his handwriting reminded me of a nervous child's in calligraphy class back in Pakistan. My parents had enrolled me in weekly lessons instead of in piano or soccer, despite my having demonstrated a strong interest in both. I doubt they would have known where to even sign me up for activities that didn't have anything to do with celebrating Islam. ("How does this make Allah happy?" they would have asked.) We would write and rewrite Arabic words, oblivious to their meaning, until they were perfectly replicated from the Quran.

The lines and curves of Nasir's letters were inconsistent, and he alternated between upper- and lowercase arbitrarily. Every *e* and *l* was curved differently each time, as if reconsidering its intent and aiming for a fresh start. Nothing about the note seemed authoritative or definitive. But I suppose there's really no right way to tell a thirteen-year-old girl she's betrothed to her first cousin.

At that age, I hadn't imagined what a potential love interest could look like for me, but Nasir certainly wasn't an obvious choice. With his thick, greasy hair that clung to his forehead, bushy eyebrows that formed a faint unibrow, and heavy moustache that hid his upper lip, he didn't resemble any of the guys in boy bands marketed to girls my age as desirable. It probably didn't help that he looked like my dad in those black-and-white photographs I'd seen in old family albums, the ones that proved my father had lived a whole other life and attracted the kind of trouble

I could only dream of before he "found the right path for Allah" and married my mom.

The truth was, I didn't know much about Nasir or my father. Getting to know men was not something the women in my family were encouraged to do. They were to be avoided at all times, like attack dogs without muzzles. In Pakistan I'd lived in a gender-segregated bubble, privy to very adult conversations among women who had created safe spaces for themselves, a private world without men. It was in those spaces that I fell in love with the beautiful, complex, and resilient beings women are. Even the most complicated woman feels uncomplicated and familiar to me. Being surrounded by sisters, aunts, and female cousins made it easy for me to not acknowledge men until I absolutely had to.

All I really knew about Nasir was that he had apparently agreed to marry me. I often wonder how that conversation took place, between him and presumably his mother. Did he resist? Was there someone he was already interested in? When he was in college in Pakistan, did he tell girls who sat next to him in class and smiled at him flirtatiously that he was arranged to marry his ten-year-old cousin and thus unavailable? And if so, did it embarrass him? Did it limit him the way it limited me? Were there hopes, dreams, and loves he couldn't pursue because his future was also decided for him? I wondered how long he had known. Did he know when he sat with us on the flight from Pakistan? Did he know when we sat together at the dining table on Sunday mornings, quietly eating breakfast with nothing to say to each other? What was going through his mind then? Was he thinking, *I'm eating with my future wife and this is what the rest of my life will look like?*

At night, Nasir would watch Bollywood videotapes—the newest ones, in which flashes of skin and heavy make-out sessions were being introduced, as opposed to the old-fashioned suggested intimacy of silhouetted embraces behind curtains. These new films were too modern for my parents. Whenever the lead actors would slowly inch closer to one another, everyone in my family would cover their eyes or fast-forward the scene. One of my parents, usually my mom, would let out an impassioned "*Astaghfirullah!*"—I seek forgiveness in Allah. At times, when someone couldn't find the remote, we would all search for it and scream "*Astaghfirullah!*" until the scene was over. You could not be a passive watcher, because passivity meant tolerance.

Hollywood movies were even more likely to feature a risqué kissing scene. In those days, my single act of rebellion was performed late at night, long after my family had gone to bed. My dad would try to fall asleep by listening to the radio, mostly Pakistani news, sometimes Urdu ghazals about loneliness caused by leaving loved ones behind. Periodically there would be commercials for Pakistani restaurants downtown or sari shops in Little India. I would wait until the radio had been turned off for a while and the entire house echoed with my dad's loud snores, then quietly sneak out of my room and watch movie trailers on the pay-per-view channel, making sure the TV was on mute. Alone, I was free to watch Sharon Stone uncross her legs in *Basic Instinct* and marvel at the scene in *Hot Shots!* when Charlie Sheen's character cools off Valeria Golino's naked body with a cube of ice. This was my version of acting inappropriately, like sneaking cigarettes or staying out past curfew.

I imagine that for Nasir, watching his favourite up-and-coming Bollywood actors display physical affection was his only brush with intimacy. But sometimes I would tell on him when he didn't fast-forward scenes that were too *haram* to watch. If I was to be policed, I would make sure that others were staying on the right path as well.

In a way, Nasir and I were complete opposites: I was trying my best to lose my accent and shed whatever branded me as different and foreign, whereas he embraced those things. It often felt as though he were stuck in a Bollywood time capsule. He dressed like Aamir Khan and Shah Rukh Khan, icons I was trying to erase from my memory and replace with new ones, in the naive hope I would then be accepted by my cruel classmates. I wished to emulate Stephanie Tanner, whose rebellious streak on the latest season of *Full House* I was extremely envious of. I was fascinated by teenagers having the luxury to learn from their mistakes, a world in which the only consequences of hanging out with the wrong crowd, taking up smoking, or making bad decisions as a result of peer pressure were grounding and detention.

In my world, every move was carefully inspected for any traces of sin, usually by my parents but also by other Muslims from the mosque who felt compelled to keep an eye on me, just as my parents kept an eye on others' children so that no one would go astray. On numerous occasions, kids from our mosque told my parents that I'd been spotted talking to boys at school, and I would have to explain to them that we were talking about homework or tests.

My parents once sent me back to the bathroom to wash off all traces of a carefully applied layer of blue eyeshadow—my dad called it *azaad*. *Azaad* is a funny word in Urdu. In most instances, it means "freedom." Freedom from your captors, war, and oppressive regimes. But when used to describe a woman, it is meant to imply that she is too wild to be tamed by those who have the right to tame her: her parents and all the men in her life whose honour it is her duty to prioritize before her desires. It's also used liberally to slut-shame and put down a woman who shows any sign of autonomy or independence.

One day I would wear the title of *azaad* like a badge of honour.

I hid Nasir's note in the pocket of my backpack and waited for my parents to return from the adult learning centre for new immigrants. My mom had plans to open up her own salon to support the family so that we could finally go off welfare. Before she could enrol in beauty school, though, she had to get her high school diploma. I would do her homework after finishing mine, since she was exhausted from her daily responsibilities.

Figuring it was the least I could do to help out, I'd taken up cooking on nights when my mom had a class. That night I'd made chicken linguini with desi spices normally used in kormas and biryanis: cumin, turmeric, and mango powder. Every non-Pakistani food I made was drenched in the spices I'd grown up with to the point that it was unfair to call it what it was inspired by. It was barely recognizable as the original. It deserved an entirely new name, or at least to have the word *desi* in front of it: desi chicken linguini, desi garlic bread, desi macaroni and cheese.

I'd also gotten into the habit of telling my mom everything. Her validation, opinions, and reactions made me feel as though we were on the same team, which meant a lot, because I was not willingly chosen by any teams at school. Even though we had different ideas about the activities and interests I was free to pursue, my mom was the only confidante I had. Keeping what I had just discovered a secret from her felt wrong. Besides, who was to say that Nasir wasn't making it all up? After all, it was my mother who had told me to be distrustful of men in the first place, on the day of my first period. The fact that she was now foisting one upon me felt like both a contradiction and a betrayal.

After dinner, as I helped her clear the table, she could tell from my body language that there was something I was dying to say. Timidly, I told her about the note and asked her whether it was true.

I could tell from her silence that Nasir hadn't made it up. I studied the golden bangles on her smooth, freshly threaded arms, watching them dip into soapy water whenever she would put a dish in the sink. She stayed silent for several minutes as I studied the side of her face, her arms, her hands, and her lowered gaze. She seemed to be searching for the right words to justify her actions. In that moment, I thought about how much I looked like her, even though relatives and family friends insisted I was a carbon copy of my dad. I looked like her most when I cried. I've only seen her cry a handful of times in my life, and each time it has broken my heart into pieces. Events that would tear people's souls and worlds apart barely elicit a raised eyebrow from my mom. It makes me wonder what kind of catastrophes she's had to endure that make deaths, disasters, and heartbreaks seem so commonplace. When I've suffered my own disappointments and looked to her for familiar compassion and comfort, the kind found in pop songs and greeting cards, I've been met with only "Baby, life is tough." Ironically, it was she, the very person who'd gotten me into this situation, who also taught me the lesson that would ultimately set me free: that we all go through hardships, tragedies, and barriers, that they're all part of life in a world that has always been incredibly unfair and cruel, but it's what we do with those experiences that allows us to leave our mark.

Eventually, my mother turned off the tap, dried her hands, and motioned for me to sit down at the kitchen table.

"Listen, Somi. I think about your best interest. You weren't supposed to know until you start university. I'm your mom. I know best."

As I stared at her, waiting for an explanation, it became clear I wasn't going to get one. And that she in fact did *not* know best—for herself or for me. Grown-ups, who are supposed to protect their children, are limited by what "best" has felt like to them, based on the circumstances they grew up in and the privilege they did or did not have. The lines between grown-up and child were often blurred between me and my mom. Her "best" did not look like mine; in fact, it looked like danger. It felt like surrender.

I wondered whether my mother ever dared to imagine what her best could look like. Did she ever have the luxury to envision a best made up of decisions that were good for her without feeling selfish and guilty? The kind of best that was truly hers and hers alone? A best that didn't make her feel that if she wasn't living for someone else's happiness, she wasn't worthy of love? A best that didn't ask her to justify her existence by being useful to others? A best that didn't ask her to mute her fire so that someone else's could burn brighter? A best that didn't require that she give away every part of herself, including her daughter, until she had nothing left? A best that didn't demand she sacrifice everything for the promise of heaven's embrace? My mother had failed to give me a better life than hers because she didn't have the blueprint to show me what my best could look like.

I had inherited the fate met by all the women in my family who came before me.

All of a sudden, the past few years started making sense. Like when my mom would open up a dream book after I'd had a nightmare and tell me what it meant. Except this was real life, and my mother had orchestrated the nightmare. Now I understood why my cousin, a simple man from a tiny village in Pakistan, had come to live with us in Canada. I had felt his permanent presence in our home as intrusive and confusing. The reality was that he was being groomed to be my husband under my parents' watchful eyes.

Shortly after that day, my parents, both my sisters, and my toddler brother were in the neighbourhood park on a summer night. I watched my siblings play as my mom joined them, but I wasn't in the mood to push anyone on the swings. I sat on a park bench and dug deep into my ice cream sundae and scooped the hot caramel from the bottom to the top, creating gold-and-white swirls with my spoon. My dad sat beside me and quietly watched. We hadn't really been close since immigrating to Canada. In fact, my siblings and I were terrified of our father. He had a bad temper that had only grown worse after the move. Anything could set him off without warning. I knew that when I truly needed him he would rise to the occasion, but I understood, as did everyone in my family, that the favour—the fatherly gestures of sympathy, care, and protection—came with a price. You had to commit to a prolonged period of obedience and assistance, like calling credit card companies and banks for better offers and lower interest rates. It would mean translating his loud demands in the background to the poor customer service reps who didn't know what vitriol would be awaiting them that day. For that reason, we didn't use the rescue card that was seemingly up for grabs whenever we needed it. We knew that our relationship with our father was always transactional. So I didn't ask him for anything. Not even to help me get out of the mess my mother had gotten me into.

After watching me for a while with uncharacteristic stillness and silence, he finally spoke. "Samra, I'm too ashamed to even talk to you about your engagement. You're still a baby," he said. "I just want to tell you that I don't agree with your mother's decision."

It was the first time my father had acknowledged the arrangement, and his words came as a surprise to me. His confession felt like an invitation to let him know if I wanted out, if I needed him to put his foot down and end my engagement with Nasir. To give him a sign that I didn't think it was okay. Then, in a rare gesture of tenderness, he put his arm around me. I held back tears and stayed still, strangely comforted by his hot breath on my face.

Although I wasn't close with my uncle, Nasir's father, I knew how much my dad looked up to him. It wasn't as simple as just saying no. Ties would be broken, relationships would be scarred, and I didn't want to be responsible for that. In my family, grudges are held for a very long time. Brothers, sisters, mothers, daughters, sons, and cousins don't speak to one another for decades over simple miscommunications, things taken a little too personally, sentiments uttered harshly, and bruised egos.

"It's okay, Dad," I said. I lied because I knew how much was at stake.

That summer, I started my first part-time job. It was at a bargain store owned by a middle-aged Saudi man and his teenage son. Neither of them would look at me when I spoke, which felt odd but also strangely comforting—if they couldn't even make eye contact, surely they would never harm me. They reminded me of my dad, who despite being loud and commanding was frightened of women who projected strength and confidence. Nothing flustered him more than a powerful female who wasn't afraid to speak her mind. At thirteen, I was already starting to realize that this was the type of woman I should aspire to be.

The store was next door to a Goodwill, where I had gone with my dad to get back-to-school clothes. I was starting ninth grade in the fall, and my bedroom wall was covered with cut-outs from Zellers flyers and catalogues: flowy silk blouses, corduroy pants, Doc Martens, plaid shirts, and vinyl trench coats that would all complement the hijab my parents insisted I start wearing when I entered high school. I was not going to let the head cover get in the way of being stylish. At the time, that seemed like a bigger challenge than it does now. Although we couldn't afford to shop at Zellers, my personal mood board guided my shopping choices at Goodwill. I had a specific look in mind to ensure that this new school year would be different for me.

I was still recovering from a social setback that past spring. I was supposed to have received a drama award at my middle-school graduation, and my mother had bought me a special outfit from a flea market for the occasion: velour bell-bottoms and an oversized T-shirt that read TAKE ME BACK TO TRINIDAD in bright red letters. I didn't have the heart to tell her I didn't want to wear it. Instead, I lied about being sick and skipped my graduation. My parents went on my behalf and reluctantly picked up my award, which remained noticeably absent from the wall of science and math awards my sisters had received. In fact, for years my nickname was Drama Award, brandished whenever I would try to get out of family obligations. It was more a taunt than a celebration of my dramatic talents, as excelling in science and math was more likely to get us out of poverty in this country than being an exceptional thespian. It wasn't exactly something my parents could brag about to relatives in Pakistan.

The truth was, I was tired of being bullied. I wanted to make friends, be accepted, and get on with my life already. So when I noticed a HELP WANTED sign in the window of the bargain store, I persuaded my dad to let me apply so that I could buy my own outfits. After learning that the owners were Muslim, my father finally agreed.

On my breaks I would scour the floor for clothes to spend my day's earnings on. I'd set aside a blue mohair sweater, a silver see-through blouse I could throw over a T-shirt, and a caramel suede jacket similar to one I'd seen in *YM* magazine. I loved organizing the suit jackets and sweaters by colour and pricing items with a pricing gun. Mostly, I was happy to be away from home—away from Nasir and the grim reality of my situation. The store wasn't far from where we lived, so I got to enjoy solitary walks through the neighbourhood, watching the sun go down and getting home just in time for dinner. It felt satisfying to know I had in some way contributed to the food my mom laid out on the dining table. And better yet, I'd acquired several new items for my wardrobe—I ended the summer perfectly poised for my reinvention.

In September I began classes at my new high school, located in one of Toronto's "high-priority" neighbourhoods, areas with a disproportionate number of low-income families and health issues and unusually high dropout rates. It was also among the most culturally diverse neighbourhoods in the city, with a large percentage of immigrants, many of whom live in subsidized housing and poverty.

I suddenly found myself surrounded by ambitious kids who were all working incredibly hard to have a life different from their parents'. Their drive was infectious, and I put in the extra effort to maintain an A average alongside them. We may not have had the latest Nikes or the newest portable CD player, but we had grades to prove we were going somewhere. Doing well in school was a matter of survival for all of us, because education was our only hope. We didn't have trust funds or parents with high-paying jobs. When I showed an interest in writing and feminism, my teachers nurtured my thirst for knowledge and recommended books by Noam Chomsky and Virginia Woolf. I was determined to get a post-secondary education and have a career, even if I was destined to be married to Nasir.

The student body at my high school was incredibly ethnically diverse. My classmates came from Italian, Jamaican, and Vietnamese families. Most of my white friends came from single-parent homes. I was no longer teased for being "other" because we were all different in our own ways. Looking different and sounding different and being different were no longer impediments to walking down the hallway or eating lunch in the cafeteria in peace.

I had started wearing the hijab, at my parents' request, but I wasn't the only one—there were dozens of girls from

India, Somalia, and Pakistan who also covered their heads. As I grew more comfortable, I would experiment on school trips, letting the silk fabric gently slide off my head and settle around my shoulders. My classmates would shriek as though I'd done something terribly shocking, then compliment me on my long curly hair. It felt good to be praised for something I admired about myself but never had the opportunity to show off. I wanted to be considered beautiful, to show that hiding underneath my hijab was hair that was just as admirable as that of other girls who put so much effort into perming, colouring, and straightening their locks. On days when my dad drove me home from school, we would often see teenage girls taking their head scarves out of their backpacks and covering their hair as they approached our apartment complex. My dad would blurt out a mocking statement that had become common among older people from the mosque—it translated to "Cover up, our people are coming." I would smile to myself, relishing the private kinship I felt with those girls.

In my first two years of high school I came out of my shell. I even started to form solid, lasting friendships. By grade eleven, Nicole and I were inseparable. She was blonde and bookish, and she invited me to things—what more could I ask for? It was gratifying that someone enjoyed my company. Because my parents could see that I was more likely to be figuring out an algebra equation with Nicole than attending a casual orgy, I was allowed to go over to her house once in a while.

One weekend, Nicole organized a dance party in her family's basement, and I told my parents I had to go over to her house to study for a math test. When I arrived her parents offered me snacks and a plastic cup of fruit punch; they asked me how the science project Nicole and I had been working on was coming along. I was shocked at how much they knew about Nicole's life and at how much support they provided her, picking her up from school and driving her to her various extracurriculars: hockey, piano lessons, softball. I excused myself, went to the bathroom, and took off my hijab. I untied my tight bun so that my hair cascaded down my shoulders and only slightly covered the Club Monaco logo on my shirt. I could hear No Doubt, mingled with the sound of laughter, as I made my way down the stairs to the candle-lit basement. Immediately I spotted Ted, a boy from my history class who was the spitting image of Kurt Cobain. He was, as though stating the obvious, wearing a Nirvana T-shirt.

"I'm not wearing a hijab," I told him, taking his cue to point out the obvious. Ted moved his shaggy hair to the side and playfully squinted his eyes as if to make sure that was what was different about me. His gesture instantly put me at ease. We were talking about how much we loved our history teacher and what we'd chosen for our essay topics when a slow song came on. Ted put down his half-finished cup of fruit punch and bashfully asked me to dance. I scanned the room so that I could mimic the moves of the other slow dancers and avoid making a fool of myself.

Ted rested his arms on my shoulders while I wrapped mine around his upper back, locking my fingers together and leaning against his chest. He smelled like fresh laundry and cherry ChapStick. He towered over me, and his blond stubble scratched against my forehead as he leaned closer, almost rocking me while we danced to a cheesy Céline Dion song.

I was sixteen, and this was the closest I had ever been to a boy in my entire life. As the song ended, we held each other for a few more seconds before disengaging. He offered me a soft smile and made his way to the snack table.

Ted, like Nicole, became a great friend—someone who made me feel safe, made me feel that I had the right to exist. By watching his animated expressions and listening to his jokes, I started learning what was considered funny among my peers and revamped my own sense of humour accordingly. By midway through high school I had watched enough North American sitcoms to get rid of my Pakistani accent, although it came back occasionally when I was worked up about something. Through practice and experience, I developed an eye for identifying the kind of people who wouldn't pick on me: smart and nerdy types who were more interested in learning about Meso-American civilizations than picking on a Pakistani girl who wore the hijab. People who devote themselves to learning have always been my people, my pockets of safety.

In spite of all this progress, and the sense of comfort I had achieved, I still wouldn't dare tell my new friends—not Nicole, not Ted—about my biggest shame: in a few months, while we would all be preparing for exams, I would be wed under Islamic law.

Weddings in my family are not the grand affairs many have come to expect from watching Bollywood movies—they're just a thing you get over with so that you can move on with your life. They're more a formality than an elaborate celebration of lives coming together, especially for immigrants, who have left their extended families and lifelong friends behind and are trying to rebuild a life for themselves. My wedding to Nasir was, in this vein, unceremonious. The lack of joy and fanfare certainly wasn't my biggest concern. Growing up, I had never fantasized about my wedding day the way girls I'd met in Canada did. For me, a wedding was an act of necessity, not a fairy tale.

My father was in London, visiting family, when my *nikah*, the Islamic marriage, took place. Although the plan had been to wait until I was eighteen, Nasir's parents were keen to have a religiously binding ceremony as soon as possible, so preparations were hastily made. I was in a daze. People from the mosque community and even the few family members who lived in Canada weren't notified, because I imagine my mother knew, on some level, that marrying off her sixteen-year-old wasn't right, even if it was technically allowed.

It was the night before my biology midterm exam, so I was anxious for the ceremony to be over. Aside from my mom and my siblings, our Iranian neighbours—a young married couple—were among the attendees. I was not happy and was making that known with my tense body language. My mother had purchased a wrinkled blue silk sari in a dusty plastic wrap a few days before in Little India. It could barely stay on my thin, angular frame. The top attached to the sari was meant for an adult woman with full breasts, not a flat-chested teenager.

Every few minutes my mom would direct me to smile for pictures, because I looked miserable. Nasir wore a boxy suit and a mismatched tie, and as we sat together he would occasionally glance at me, perhaps hoping that I would give him, if not some indication that he was the love of my life, then at the very least a smile. I felt a recurring pang in my stomach. I wasn't sure how I was supposed to feel, but I was pretty sure wanting to burst into tears wasn't it.

For years afterwards, my mother would remind me of how I signed the *nikah* papers that night without any hesitation. The fact that I didn't resist was an indication that I was okay with the arrangement, and this belief absolved her of guilt and shifted some of the accountability onto me. That particular detail and her memory of it would haunt me as I tried to undo the damage it caused. I started to internalize my mother's belief that my lack of resistance was my way of consenting and that I was responsible for what had happened. I carried the guilt within me, holding myself accountable for not saying anything earlier, even though I felt that I couldn't.

And so, at sixteen, I was a teenage bride, and the *nikah* was the chastity belt I wore to guard me from the temptation of teenage rebellion in a country that had given me my first taste of freedom.

five

The story of how my parents met begins with this undisputed fact: my father is a terrible driver. He is fast, reckless, and impatient. He should never have been allowed to drive a car. My childhood in Pakistan consisted of me ducking in the back seat whenever my dad picked me up from school because he would almost hit drivers on his way out of the parking lot and get into screaming matches with other fathers, usually in Punjabi, which has a broader vocabulary of vulgarity than Urdu.

The day he met my mother, my dad side-swiped a woman while speeding. She was injured and bleeding, and he picked her up and took her to the hospital. When he arrived, a family friend advised him to leave before the police came. He fled to his sister's, his white kurta covered in blood. My mom happened to be at his sister's house that day, and when she saw him, she assumed he'd been hurt and helped him clean up. Soon after that encounter my dad made his interest in my mom known to her family, and a few months later, they were married.

They were a mismatched couple: my father was as loud and uncensored as my mother was fragile and sensitive, carrying around the trauma from her past. Because of her class, she didn't have many options to leave her burdened life. Until she met my father.

Growing up, I never witnessed my parents utter "I love you" to each other. Perhaps that's why I hadn't asked my dad for help when he seemed to offer me a way out of my engagement with Nasir. At the time, I didn't know that loving someone was an essential ingredient of marriage. I'm sure my parents love and care for each other deeply in ways that aren't always apparent to me. They are very much codependent, and they argue all the time, mostly about my mom's spending habits. Whenever my mom is feeling especially down, she scours the aisles of beauty departments and home decor stores to temporarily ease the pain of whatever it is she's going through: problems with her health, fights with my dad, loneliness. As a result, every available surface in my parents' bedroom and bathroom is cluttered with unopened moisturizers, serums, oils, body washes, and hair dyes—all products that promise a release from self-discontent. But some days, observing them together on the sofa, two middle-aged people sitting side by side, my dad with his pot-belly he refused to do anything about and my mom with her unnaturally burgundy hair, watching Pakistani talk shows on satellite, they seemed imperfectly perfect together.

Even at sixteen, freshly married to Nasir, I knew that future wasn't for me.

By the time I entered grade twelve, I was gravitating more than ever to images and pop-culture reference points that promised a much more appealing life than my own—a fantasy world where girls were allowed to be playful, expressive, and free. A place for people who were curious and always seeking answers. My locker and bedroom walls were plastered with pictures of the Spice Girls, United Colors of Benetton ads, and pages carefully torn from *i-D* magazine. But in my reality, there were limitations to how much I could pursue an individual identity, because my identity had already been decided for me.

There were, however, unexpected perks to being married. For one, my parents were less strict about policing my appearance. I could wear lipsticks that had names like espresso, mocha, and dark chocolate to school without being scolded for wanting to attract boys' attention.

The truth was, I wasn't wearing it for the boys.

In the change room I would watch in awe as girls who felt completely comfortable with their full nakedness, as though they'd never been told to cover up before, talked about boys they had fucked or wanted to fuck. I stole glances at their breasts and witnessed their overt sexuality with a mix of fear and excitement. I had no idea women could actively seek out sex and enjoy it—or, even more shockingly, brag about it. I thought sex was something that was done *to* women. (My mother had made it sound painful, not at all pleasurable.) I didn't dare divulge that I didn't have any updates on who I wanted to kiss, let alone sleep with, because I was married to my first cousin.

But my curiosity had been piqued. Even though we were married, so far Nasir and I had not been physical with each other. At seventeen, I'd never been kissed. Now more than ever I wanted to know what it felt like. I may not have been attracted to Nasir, but there was a certain thrill in having permission to explore my sexuality with someone and not get in trouble for it. He was my husband, after all; it wasn't *haram*. I wouldn't have been as bold and comfortable with someone from school, because wearing the hijab made me feel undesirable. Although it was strange to be kissing the man who symbolized everything I was bristling against, I was just starting to understand the sexual power my body possessed, and it was exciting. I didn't know that I could enjoy feeling desired or that I could be the object of someone's lust. I thought I was too skinny and that my breasts were too small, not at all like the full, round ones I'd seen in the change room.

By then Nasir had moved out of our house and into an apartment building near the mosque. My parents wanted us to wait until I finished high school before we started living together as husband and wife. But we were allowed to talk on the phone and spend time together, which I would never have been able to do with another boy. I would meet him in his rusted Toyota during lunch hour, and we would drive to a nearby park to make out. I remember being more excited by the act of sneaking around than I was by feeling his lips on my neck or his fingers tracing my thighs. In those fumbling moments I learned how erotic restraint could be. I wasn't interested in sex, which Nasir and I never had. What excited me was the anticipation, and afterwards savouring every detail from our time together. I would tell him where I wanted to feel his touch: below my breasts, above my hips, the back of my neck and ears. I could tell that he was as inexperienced as I was.

At that age, I was scarcely prepared for becoming sexually active. Among my other blind spots, I had no idea it was impossible to get pregnant without removing one's pants. I certainly couldn't rely on my mother for any sort of sex education. So when a missed period sent me into a panic, it took a frank anatomy lesson from my gym teacher, Ms. McLean, to calm me down. Although I was embarrassed by my confession, I didn't have anyone else in my life I could turn to—no one to listen without judgment. Gone were the days when I could tell my mom everything.

It wasn't the first time Ms. McLean had come to my rescue. Earlier that year, she had saved me from drowning in the shallow end of the school swimming pool as I attempted my very first swim. I was weighed down by my sweatsuit and hijab, which my parents insisted I wear in the water during lessons. I was the only girl in the shallow end, so it took a few minutes for others to notice what was happening before Ms. McLean was splashing through the water to bring me to the surface. After that incident, my parents were willing to compromise and let me swim in a bathing suit, so long as I put on my hijab right after I left the change room.

Swimming became a refuge for me, one of the few liberating activities in my life, and I swam whenever I had the opportunity. To this day, I associate the smell of chlorine with the freedom I found in that pool, letting my body move any way it wanted, bringing my knees close to my chest and floating weightlessly. Here, my body wasn't a problem; it wasn't a cause for alarm or a tool to excite men—here I could simply *be*. By the end of the school year I no longer feared the deep end.

———

In contrast to my parents' newfound leniency, Nasir had begun to police my behaviour. One of the ways he did so was to closely examine the books I borrowed from the library and piled high on my nightstand. Nasir wanted to make sure that nothing was polluting my mind, encouraging me to be a *kaafir*, a disbeliever. He was threatened by my education and its potential to create a power imbalance between us. Literature in English made him particularly wary, as it might instill in my head ideas he had no control over. Unlike my mom, he didn't see any benefit in my getting an education, and he made his views known.

Growing up as sheltered as I had, books provided a much-needed window into worlds I would never experience. They could afford me the comfort, safety, adventure, and glamour that I didn't have access to but so deeply craved. I could travel anywhere in the world, even if in my real life I was barely allowed to leave the house. My dad would have to force me to stop reading at night so that he could turn off the light and let my sister, whom I shared a room with, finally sleep. Once he was gone, I would take my book out from under the covers and squint to make out the words by the light of my digital alarm clock.

Having outgrown the Nancy Drew novels of my early teens, I had moved on to Margaret Atwood and Agatha Christie. Sometimes I would even sneak in erotica by Nora Roberts. I was delighted that in only a few years, my

English had improved so much that the language could help me get turned on.

I loved being surrounded by books so much that I started working at the school library. After my summer job at the bargain store had ended, I needed pocket money to pay for clothes and makeup I would see in the magazines I browsed during lunch hour: *YM*, *Seventeen*, *Sassy*, *Tiger Beat*. With my very first library paycheque I purchased a white latex trench coat from Le Château. I would wear it year-round, even when it was scorching hot out. I figured if I had to dress modestly and cover myself, I might as well look chic doing it. I loved the compliments and attention I received when I wore it, pleased I hadn't purchased something safe or boring. During slow days at the library I even painted my nails with Wite-Out so that they matched my coat.

I would bring bags full of books home and stack them by my single bed, as though arranging presents under the Christmas tree, soon to be opened up. Periodically, I would notice that certain books had disappeared, usually after Nasir had paid a visit. Soon enough, I was confronted by my mother and Nasir about reading books that he thought were putting impure thoughts in my head. He had highlighted words that he found problematic: *sex*, *kissing*, and *love*. I'm sure there'd have been even more yellow on the pages if his English had been better.

I was in disbelief. Here I was getting in trouble, not for staying out late, hanging with the wrong crowd, or doing drugs, but for reading! I felt as though the window to the outside world I so treasured was being boarded up.

After that day, I made sure to hide the books I brought home, and I took them out only once my bedroom door was locked. Books became my dirty little secrets, my illicit, hidden contraband.

In my final year of high school, my relationship with Nasir worsened. One day, my mom told me that a female relative had been physically assaulted by her husband after an argument and was seeking separation. The news travelled fast, and within a few hours, all the relatives knew. I was shaken. Although instances of physical and psychological abuse in my family weren't anything new, such stories would always make me anxious about what the future held for me.

By my late teens I'd witnessed many violent arguments between my parents. Years after moving to Canada, my father's inability to provide for our family financially remained a hotly contentious issue. Whenever they fought I would lock myself in my room, holding on to my little brother tightly and covering his ears. If I was alone, I would drown out the screams and shouts by putting on headphones and listening to soothing music. Philip Glass or Mozart would provide the soundtrack as a war waged outside my door.

When I felt absolutely hopeless, I would turn to Allah for guidance. If it weren't for having to read the Quran every day since as far back as I could remember, I would have believed I didn't deserve to be happy, to be loved, or to have a choice in who I married. I would have spent my entire life believing that violence was just a given, a reality I had no choice but to tolerate. But Allah, my Allah, told me that I deserved better. So I would pray to him when I felt that no one was looking out for me in this world, not even my parents. *O Messenger of Allah! It is a great Mercy of God that you are gentle and kind toward them; for, had you been harsh and hard-hearted, they would all have broken away from you.* As long as I was kind, like the Prophet Muhammad, I could have the life I imagined when I closed my eyes—a life where I would come home from school to a warm meal and parents who were proud of me no matter how I chose to express my true, unvarnished self.

Naively I turned to Nasir for comfort. I was shocked to discover his stance on the physical abuse our relative had suffered. "I can see it being necessary on some occasions," he said. Even before my mother picked up to tell us that our time to talk for the day was up, I hung up on him, having made up my mind that there was no way I could ever stay with someone who thought it was okay to hit his wife. I refused to repeat the cycle of abuse and violence that had plagued the women in my family.

I wanted a different kind of life. A life where I wasn't afraid. A life where I didn't have to ask for a man's permission to read, to go to university, to drive a car. But I feared that the feminist ideals I had learned from books, teachers, and peers at school wouldn't register with my parents. Besides, Nasir and I were already married. I knew how messy things would get, especially because we were family. What would people say? In my parents' minds, breaking up the *nikah* would permanently label me as difficult, tainted, broken. No one would ever want to marry me after that. It was too late.

For months I dodged Nasir, ignoring his requests to talk on the phone. Instead I focused on my other life—the life that didn't involve him, where I felt safe, where I was flourishing. I was happier shelving books at work, joking around with friends at study groups, and making my teachers proud by excelling in English literature, history, and world politics. I just wanted to be told that I was worthy, I was smart and I deserved good things happening to me. When one of my favourite teachers suggested I might consider a career as a diplomat, I was ecstatic. It was validating to know that despite my voice being muted at home, people I respected believed in me and were rooting for me.

Foolishly, I asked my father to come with me to a parent-teacher meeting. I was proud of how I was performing in all my classes and wanted my dad to hear it from one of my teachers, so that he'd know I wasn't just a "drama student." My math teacher beamed with pride as he told my father how well I'd done on a recent test.

"Oh this is nothing," my father replied. "You should meet my younger daughter, way smarter!" I avoided meeting my teacher's eyes for weeks.

My younger sisters went to school in a different part of the city—a school for students who were gifted in math and sciences and came from families that didn't have to worry about money. It always felt as though their education was more of a priority than mine because my parents knew that I would be married off anyway.

Staying at school even after the final bell rang was the only way I could cope with life. I joined clubs and committees, tutored younger students, and told my parents I was studying at the library when in fact I was attending after-school dances in the gymnasium. At those dances, I felt empowered to reveal my other side, the fun-loving teenager I wasn't allowed to be in front of my parents. The girl who secretly listened to Notorious B.I.G. and TLC in her bedroom, memorizing all the lyrics so she could sing along with her friends on the dance floor. Under the makeshift disco lights, I would take off my hijab and dance, flipping my hair, free to be my unadulterated self.

Sensing he was losing his control over me, Nasir resorted to desperate measures. He called the school's main switchboard and got the number for the library. Whenever he called, I would tell him I was busy and hang up. I did not want to engage with him in any way. Then he started showing up at the school, waiting for me in the parking lot and offering me a ride home.

I knew there was no point trying to reason with him about domestic abuse. It would open a can of worms; I would be exposed to even more problematic opinions that he'd never had to question or examine because he lacked awareness and the language. In Pakistan, where Nasir came of age, there's a stigma surrounding conversations about sexism and domestic abuse, and women's basic rights are still largely ignored. Nor could I tell my parents why I was dodging Nasir's phone calls. Citing sexism would be met with blank stares and indifference. I knew that since he hadn't acted violently toward me, they wouldn't see any cause for concern.

I would need to find my own way out.

With a semester left till graduation, it seemed I may have found my ticket out in Peter, the boy I'd asked to the senior prom. Peter and I had met back in grade eleven English class. I took quick notice of him: the way his gentle eyes creased when he smiled, his honey-brown skin and defined jaw. His parents had emigrated from South Africa to escape the oppressive grip of apartheid, and his dad was the only person of colour in their small town. Although Peter was born in Canada, he was very much aware of his status as other, growing up largely among white children. After his parents separated, he was raised by his white mother. Instead of verbalizing his feelings about his parents' separation and the racism he faced, Peter became a recluse, finding solace in nature, especially fishing. Stifled by the lack of adventure in his town, he started acting out. His parents decided he needed a father figure in his life, so he moved to Toronto to live with his dad.

I've always been drawn to loners, people who have the strength not to join the herd just for validation. Over the course of grades eleven and twelve, we'd slowly come to know each other better. We bonded over our flawed parents and painful upbringings; although we'd been scarred by our experiences in different ways, our empathy for each other's childhood trauma brought us closer together. He shared with me the dark poetry he'd written about his father and growing up in the small town, and that made me want to take care of him and give him love. I felt safer and more comfortable in Peter's company than in my parents' or Nasir's. Until

I met Peter, every male in my life had been controlling. I had internalized that their need to control me was something I simply had to accept—that it was the price I had to pay for being a woman. But with Peter I felt safe enough to reveal that I was married to my cousin. I made it clear that it was not a decision I had made for myself, and that I intended to get out of it. I was relieved when he was understanding and almost protective of me. Until then, I believed that escaping my arranged marriage would leave a permanent scar, branding me undesirable and unworthy of love. My fear wasn't unfounded—I'd seen women in Pakistan who had left their husbands and were met with judgment, accusation, and hushed gossip. But Peter changed my mind.

One afternoon we skipped class and went to the apartment he shared with his dad. He showed me his dingy bedroom, where dark, thick curtains obstructed any natural light. Unfolded clothes spilled out of drawers, and the miniature Dungeons & Dragons figurines he was painting took over his entire desktop—a tiny universe of his own creation. Peter put on one of his mixtapes, and we made out to the music of Leonard Cohen, Smashing Pumpkins, and Lenny Kravitz, artists he'd introduced me to over the past year. It was exhilarating to be kissing someone I actually liked, instead of my husband.

Afterwards, he heated a can of tomato soup on the stove and brought me a bowl. We didn't eat canned food at home, so this was an exotic treat. Peter sat across from me and quietly watched, amused, as I slurped the hot soup, savouring every mouthful. He said he was amazed how regal I could look while eating a can of cheap soup. That I looked like a queen being served at her castle. I waved as though I were the queen of England.

I asked Peter if he wanted to be my boyfriend. He was surprised I'd even asked him to the prom. He motioned to the pink silk hijab draped across the back of my chair and said he'd assumed I would never be allowed to attend. I told him not to worry, and got up to kiss him goodbye.

Of course I lied to my parents about the prom, telling them it was a graduation party. They had heard about the prom from their friends at the mosque, who told them to be cautious because the students were usually unsupervised and got up to no good. My mom was a little surprised when we went shopping for my "graduation party" dress and I picked out a low-cut baby blue spaghetti-strap number. I assured her I would wear a jacket overtop and that I just liked the hit of colour.

When the night of the prom finally arrived, I was giddy with excitement. But my excitement quickly faded when I realized my father was waiting in the parking lot of the banquet hall a mere hour after dropping me off. I had to wonder if he'd even left at all. I'd danced with Peter and my friends to only one song before it was time for me to leave. My friends looked confused, as they often did when I gave them the abridged version of my complicated life. I went to the bathroom to put my hijab back on before hurrying out to my dad's car.

In the days following the prom I plunged deeper into despair. I felt cornered, with nowhere to turn for help, no one to ask for advice. Although Peter cared for me, he wasn't equipped to help me safely exit my marriage. I was starting to entertain thoughts of suicide, which in my distraught state was beginning to seem like the only option. After seeing an ad on a cereal box, I called a youth hotline from a telephone booth. It was as if the counsellor at the other end had never encountered my specific situation—a teenage Muslim girl trapped in an unhappy arranged marriage—and when she suggested I tell my parents how I felt, I hung up on her.

That night, Nasir brought me a breaded veal sandwich after his shift at the 7-Eleven—his attempt at a romantic gesture. I was repulsed by the way it smelled and looked; I wanted nothing to do with it, just like our marriage. I took the sandwich into the kitchen, where I discreetly doused it in bleach. In that moment, I truly believed that harming myself was the only way I could escape my circumstances.

After taking a few bites, I started to feel dizzy and nauseated. Nasir and my mom were in the living room watching a Bollywood soap opera. I told them I wasn't feeling well and needed to see a doctor right away. Nasir drove us to the clinic in his Toyota, and I sat in the back seat with my head out the window, feeling the brisk air on my face. As sweat dripped down my back, I promised myself that if I didn't die that night, I would get myself out of the situation any way I could. After an hour in the waiting room, my symptoms started to dissipate. Nervous that I'd have to come clean with the doctor about my actions, I told my mom and Nasir I was feeling well enough to leave.

Back home, I asked everyone to gather in my parents' bedroom. There, I announced that I did not love Nasir. I said I was sure that one day he would make someone very happy, but that someone wasn't going to be me. He threatened to tell my parents about what we did together, implying we'd had sex and knowing that would discourage my parents from letting me end the marriage because it would mean I was no longer pure. I told him I didn't care, that it wasn't true.

My mom suggested that we give Nasir a makeover, as if this would solve everything. To her, his lack of style was his only shortcoming.

I'm not sure how I summoned the courage to say that nothing could change my mind. I did not want to be Nasir's wife, and that was that. I no longer felt scared to share what I had been feeling for years. In fact, for the first time in my life, I felt brave. I finally knew how it felt to stand by my convictions, unconcerned about the consequences.

The room was silent. No one knew what to say or do.

Nasir left, and I never saw him again. Just like that, he was extinguished from my life. In the coming weeks, the mosque annulled our *nikah*, crystallizing the end of our brief and rocky union.

I thought life would become bearable once Nasir was gone, but if anything, my parents became more cruel and controlling. Before the annulment, I could at least live peacefully under the guise of the good, obedient Muslim girl. Now my parents saw that I was rebellious and in need of discipline. They reverted to their old ways, monitoring my every move, looking for clues as to why I had ended my marriage.

In desperate need of an outlet for my anger and frustration, I made a rash decision: I cut off all my hair. Inspired by the strong female pop stars of the time—Pink, Toni Braxton, Dolores O'Riordan of the Cranberries—I transformed myself by shedding the long, dark locks I'd once been so proud of.

In the aftermath of my suicide attempt, I needed guidance from Allah more than ever. I would accompany my mom to the mosque, as I always had, but soon enough, as word spread that I was a rebellious daughter who had broken off her *nikah*, the aunties began accusing my mom of doing a terrible job raising me. I could tolerate accusations directed at me (I was used to it by then), but I felt incredibly protective of my parents. I didn't want them to be ridiculed and embarrassed in a place that brought them so much joy, their only community.

The mothers of my old friends at the mosque advised them to no longer talk to me. They didn't want my rebellion to rub off on their daughters. Ostracized, I started praying alone at home.

Back at school, I kept the details of my tumultuous home life a secret from my friends and classmates, including Peter. As we prepared to say our goodbyes and begin the next chapter of our lives, I was bracing myself for an even bigger transition. I had received acceptance letters to all the universities I had applied to, including the best journalism program in the country. I had also been approved for a student loan, which would help pay my tuition, although I would still have to find a part-time job to cover other basic necessities. I was constantly fighting with my parents about my desire to attend journalism school and to live closer to campus. I understood that continuing to live under their roof would mean being made to feel guilty about ending my marriage and being reminded, every day, what a bad Muslim I was.

Peter had recently moved into a basement apartment after saving up enough money from his job as a prep cook at a steakhouse. He had always been an exceptional cook, and working at the restaurant would help him realize his dream of becoming a chef. After a particularly nasty argument with my parents, I asked him if I could stay with him until I figured out my next steps. To my relief, he said yes.

Early one August morning, I made my move—a move that would forever change the course of my life and my relationship with my parents. While my family was still asleep, I gathered a few sweaters to get me through the chilly fall days, my white latex trench coat, my collection of lipsticks, and the identification cards my dad kept in a drawer. I left all my hijabs behind except for the pink silk one. I snuck into their bedrooms and kissed my younger sisters and my kid brother goodbye. Knowing that my father is a light sleeper, I closed the front door without making a sound. I walked away and didn't look back.

six

I felt like I was in hiding. Even after moving my meagre possessions into Peter's basement apartment on the outskirts of the city, the space still felt like a temporary refuge. But I took comfort in the fact that I was seizing control of my life. Sure, there was mould in the walls, and very little natural light, but the rent was cheap and the landlord didn't care that his tenant had just moved his girlfriend in. I threw a vintage fur coat over a cardboard box to create a makeshift vanity table—I could still cling to the illusion of glamour even if my reality was devoid of it.

To earn some extra money, I got a part-time job at the Body Shop. I was surrounding myself in beauty products—soaps that smelled of orange blossom, peppermint foot creams—just as my mother had. Peter, now working as a cook at a family-owned Italian restaurant, covered most of the living expenses. For someone who'd just walked away from a marriage, I was stepping into a very marriage-like arrangement—a sort of dress rehearsal for adulthood.

Peter was unlike any other man I'd ever met: gentle and non-threatening. I knew implicitly that he would never hurt me. He was never jealous or angry, and his indifference, his dispassion, felt like safety to me. It was all I needed.

As the summer came to an end, I anxiously anticipated my freshman orientation at Ryerson University. Having been sheltered for so long, I didn't feel quite ready. I barely knew how to take the bus downtown; I barely knew where downtown *was*! But I was determined to put my best foot forward. I'd stopped wearing my hijab, and my close-cropped hair was on full display to the world—at least I could project a street-smart aura, even if I felt like a scared little kid. I scoped out my fellow journalism majors as we waited to be let into our first Introduction to Reporting lecture. There, among the pockets of white women who avoided eye contact with me and the jocks with their frosted tips, was Andrew. He was wearing a bright linen shirt under a caramel cashmere sweater and the kind of slouchy plaid wool trousers I'd only ever seen on *Fashion Television*. He held a leather portfolio bag that looked as soft as butter. He was ready for life, and I wanted to go along. I don't know what came over me in that moment, but I walked up and introduced myself to this man who dared to express his inherent elegance in a sea of hot-pink bejewelled Juicy Couture tracksuits. I was instantly comforted by the warmth and eagerness with which he received my introduction. We sat next to each other in class, and just like that, I'd made my first new friend.

As I poured myself into my course work, my old life began to feel more distant. And yet I was constantly being reminded of all that I'd left behind in the form of tearful voicemails from my mom. Other than to go to school, I had barely left the house for more than a few hours in my life, and this new, protracted absence was more than she could bear. For months she called my cell phone several times a day, pleading with me to let her know I was still alive. Sometimes I too would cry as I listened to her messages, but other times I'd just stare into space, picking lint off my tights or scraping polish off my nails as she talked about how not knowing where I was made her want to die.

When her crying finally became too much, and the sheen of my anger had worn off, I called her. I lay on the bed left behind by the previous tenant and clutched the phone in my sweaty hand, my heart thumping. She picked up after one ring.

"Somi? Where are you? Are you okay?"

"I'm fine, Mom," I said. "I can't tell you where I am."

"Are you living with a boy?"

"Yes."

"Is this boy your boyfriend?"

I paused. I'd thought that by running away I'd drawn a line in the sand: I didn't have to answer to my parents anymore. It was a radical and irreversible act of rebellion. But in that moment, I wanted to spare my mother the pain of knowing that I was "living in sin"—her deepest fear realized. (In fact, my guilt was so strong that I still hadn't even had sex with Peter.)

So I lied. I told her Peter and I had eloped. I could hear her relief. I answered her barrage of questions with one-word replies. She wanted to know all the details—where we'd been married, what I had worn, if anyone from the mosque had seen us together, if she could see the marriage certificate—and beneath her questions I sensed a creeping suspicion, as though she knew I was lying. I was frustrated with myself for still not being free of her hold. I had thought I was now independent, but it took only one phone call to learn that I was still my mother's child. Eager to end the conversation before I revealed too much, I agreed that Peter and I would meet her for dinner the following week.

My mother showed up to the restaurant bearing gifts for Peter, with my youngest sister in tow. I suppose she was grateful that someone out there was willing to take her already divorced teenage daughter as his wife. Peter pulled a cream cable-knit sweater and khaki pants out of the Gap shopping bag. Perhaps my mother thought she could fix Peter the same way she thought she could fix Nasir: with a makeover. What were her criteria for an ideal mate for her daughter anyway? Which shortcomings could be corrected and which could be accommodated by lowering expectations?

We ordered our meals, and my mother asked Peter about his job as a cook. She had a difficult time grasping the fact that a man would choose to perform a role traditionally associated with women. Cooking food was one of Peter's only pleasures in life, aside from fishing and smoking, but my mother couldn't comprehend how it could ever bring him joy.

My father had stubbornly refused to join us. To him, my marrying a non-Muslim meant a guaranteed entry to hell, and he would have no part of it. I thought back to the sensationalist news stories we'd sometimes see on television, about Muslim fathers who disciplined their disobedient daughters through extreme measures, sometimes even killing them for muddying the family honour. My father used to talk to me about how misguided those men were; I knew he could never do anything like that, even if in moments of rage he threatened he might. But the father I'd known in Pakistan had faded away long ago, so his absence that night didn't feel unusual. I'd taken a baby step with my mom, but it would take a marathon to cross the divide with my father.

———

That winter, in our third month of pretend marriage, I asked Peter if he would *actually* marry me. We'd jokingly talked about taking that final leap toward putting my parents' mind at ease, but along the way the boundary between charade and reality became blurred. Peter, a little startled, said yes. Suddenly I was engaged for a second time, and I wasn't even twenty.

We didn't waste any time making the arrangements— once again, the wedding would be quick and unceremonious. On our way to city hall, we stopped to buy our wedding bands at a jewellery store run by a Persian couple. I picked a white gold ring that choked my bony finger. (The woman behind the counter told Peter to make sure it was too tight to ever come off, as though I weren't standing right there.) Instead of asking for a different size, I just smiled and handed over my credit card.

I wore a pink blouse and the black pencil skirt I'd worn for my interview at the Body Shop, with a magenta hair extension I'd bought at the mall for a final flourish. Peter wore a blue dress shirt tucked into black slacks—he looked like a kid masquerading as a grown-up. Peter's friend Mike and Mike's girlfriend, Mae, acted as our witnesses. We celebrated by going to a steakhouse close to city hall.

All through dinner, a spectre was looming: even though we'd been living together for more than six months, Peter and I still hadn't had sex. I'd overheard my female co-workers talk about giving their boyfriends blow jobs in parked cars, but I had no desire to do anything like that with Peter. I wondered if there was something wrong with me. Now that we were married, there was an expectation, and I no longer had the convenience of Muslim guilt to protect me from the last thing I wanted to do: have sex with my husband.

Afterwards we went to a dive bar where Peter was a regular. I unclipped my hair extension and put it in my backpack and searched for quarters to play "No Scrubs" on the jukebox. I asked the Vietnamese owner which cocktails she recommended, because I'd only recently turned nineteen and had never ordered a drink before. She eased me in with fruity concoctions: Sex on the Beach and piña coladas. Whenever Peter ran into the people he saw every night after his shifts, he introduced me as his wife. I was as shocked by the sound of it as they were.

We were tipsy by the time we got home. Anxious to get it over with, I removed the white garter belt and bustier I'd bought after Peter mentioned he was into lingerie. I tensed up as he entered me, sending a jolt of pain through my body. I asked him to stop. He got off me and we lay on our backs, staring up at the ceiling. I was puzzled. Wasn't sex supposed to be pleasurable and exciting? Even though I hadn't been looking forward to it, I'd hoped I would miraculously start to love it once I finally gave in. We tried again in the morning, and this time I didn't tell him to stop. When it was over, I saw that blood had dripped down my legs and onto my white stockings. I crumpled them into a ball and threw them in the garbage before I left for work.

Peter was just as inexperienced as I was when it came to sex, but it was clear that he wanted it. I, on the other hand, was convinced I was asexual. I'd fleetingly enjoyed being desired by Nasir, but those feelings had evaporated once they led to his presumption of ownership over me. Now, songs with lyrics that alluded to lust, longing, and passion didn't resonate with me. Sex was a chore, like paying bills or washing dishes. The satisfaction was not in the act itself but in the result: no overdue bills, a clean kitchen. A happy husband. The fact was that I didn't desire Peter—or any other man, for that matter. So, night after night, I said no.

While one part of me was shutting down, another part was coming to life. My blossoming friendship with Andrew was a lesson in giving myself permission to envision a future and possibilities that otherwise might not have been extended to me. My request for a casual coffee catch-up between midterms yielded an invitation to the Four Seasons, where wait staff in crisp white shirts asked if he'd like his usual seat. We were always the youngest people in the room, but Andrew never looked out of place anywhere we went. From his trips, he brought me beautiful gifts, like an Italian Murano glass ring in my favourite shade of green. Recognizing my preference for oversized silhouettes—a nod to the burkas my mother wore—he took me to Holt Renfrew and encouraged me to try on garments in similar shapes by Comme des Garçons and Marni, even though I couldn't afford them. But as personal shoppers brought me dresses in beautiful fabrics and striking colours, I felt I had as much right to be there as anyone else. There is power in giving off the aura of belonging. Maybe Andrew saw a vision of my future self that I was still blind to.

Together we dared to imagine a beautiful life, and we sought it through fashion, art, and film. We developed a secret language of joint smirks and shared glances, always seeking out the most interesting person in the room—the one who seemed just a little offbeat and out of place and had the best, most interesting stories. Andrew appreciated digging deeper for meaning and always emphasized the importance of pausing to just look, savour, and listen when the world demanded that. (One night, while driving me home from a party thrown by art school kids, he stopped his car on top of a hill that glistened from a recent downpour and switched off the engine. I checked the passenger side mirror, wondering if there was a police car behind us. The night was very still, and there were no other cars on the road. Then Andrew turned up the stereo and pushed back the driver's seat to enjoy the first minute of Madonna's "Vogue" before he sat up, started the engine, and drove on.) He noted the things that went largely unnoticed: a point of view not considered in the chorus of arguments; the quiet, relatively unknown performers overlooked in movie reviews; people who worked behind the scenes in every art form and were just as deserving of the thunderous applause; socialites who dared to make their international pop music debut and were cool to hate. Maybe I was also an underdog he was rooting for.

Emboldened by this new way of seeing myself, I became a little more adventurous with my look. I started going to a salon downtown that resembled a spaceship, where you were given an asymmetrical mullet no matter what you asked for and Depeche Mode and New Order blasted over the speakers. Inspired by the feeling of ownership over my body, I got my first tattoo, of the Japanese word for beauty (my fascination with the country and culture had only grown since ESL class with Ms. Nakamura). I felt a flicker of buried guilt as the tool pierced my skin, knowing that tattoos are forbidden in Islam. But by the time it healed, I was already thinking about what I'd get for my second.

I'd started using LiveJournal and connected with a group of young feminist women of colour who were a bit older than me and had started their careers, mostly in media. Meeting people online was one of the few ways I could form connections with people I had something in common with. Alienated from my family and the mosque community, I'd become intensely aware of the lack of people of colour in my life and was trying to remedy that. I was certain that by doing so I would find comfort and finally be understood in my entirety.

That summer, after weeks of exchanging ideas and messages online, some of the women made plans to meet for a picnic in a park. I showed up late from an afternoon shift at the Body Shop and added the container of mush-room pasta with congealed rosé sauce I'd picked up from the grocery store to their array of gluten-free and vegan offerings. I quickly learned that although the group was strictly for women of colour, I was the only one who was not born in Canada. Many of them had the emotional and financial support of their parents, who had well-paying jobs and had never had to struggle with a language barrier.

"What are some of the biggest challenges you've had to confront as a person of colour?" the ringleader, a brown girl with a Sleater-Kinney T-shirt, asked the group. One by one, the others in the circle shared how instances of racism and sexism had prevented them from getting the same opportunities in their careers as their peers. I straightened my back, which ached from being on my feet all day at the shop. The privilege of being second or even third generation wasn't lost on me.

By the time it was my turn to speak, I could feel myself shaking; I wondered if my voice would betray me. But I couldn't bring myself to sugar-coat it. "I guess the biggest challenges I've faced are escaping my arranged marriage and dealing with the fear that I'll have to go on welfare like my parents," I said, pulling blades of grass from the wet ground, not quite able to look any of the girls in the eye. Everyone was quiet, as if unsure what to say. Weighed down by their silence and inability to connect, I felt even more isolated.

My mother's beauty salon had grown into a kind of a community drop-in centre for Pakistani women in her neighbourhood. Not only was she able to bring in money to support the family, but she also employed other Pakistani women who would work the reception desk, wax clients' eyebrows, faces, arms, and legs, and occasionally, if my mother trusted them enough, cut and colour their hair.

The salon became a convenient place for me to reconnect with my mother, since my father rarely made an appearance there. I imagine he was intimidated by how outspoken and opinionated women became in the absence of the men in their lives, by the frankness and ease with which they talked about their husbands and the creepy white men who came in to hit on them. His presence would be swept under the roar of their spontaneous laughter. At the salon, women he didn't know had created their own universe. They made their own decisions and dared one another to express themselves through over-the-top hairdos, persuading each other to get extra-bright highlights because that was the *rawaj*, the trend back in Pakistan. They released the pent-up loud laughter that at home made Allah so unhappy. My father was no one to them and couldn't tell them what to do. So he resigned himself to waiting outside in the car when it was time to pick my mother up and take her back home, the place where he reigned.

Despite her disapproval of the choices I'd made, whenever I walked through the door of her salon, my mother would introduce me with pride. "Everyone, this is my punk daughter, Samra," she'd announce to the women in hijabs and burkas waiting to get their eyebrows threaded or for their hair to be shaped into chignons for their daughters' weddings. I didn't know where this newfound pride had stemmed from (or, for that matter, where she'd learned the word *punk*), but I wondered if, by breaking myself out of the cycle that had imprisoned her and so many other women in my family, I had also freed her. The bolder and more experimental I became with my fashion—inspired by such designers as Rei Kawakubo and Ann Demeulemeester and icons like Patti Smith—the more excited she became. I was her window into a thrilling new world.

The wounds still hadn't completely healed, but little by little, we reimagined our relationship at a time when we were both experiencing our first taste of autonomy. Over time my mother made peace with the fact that I no longer wore the hijab, and I came to look forward to hanging out with her in the salon. Sometimes during those visits her eyes would well up, as if she still couldn't believe that I had come back after disappearing from her life. She'd start to tell me how she roamed the hallways of my high school like a madwoman, knocked on the doors of everyone I'd ever mentioned casually in conversation, and visited every library in the neighbourhood looking for me. "Mom, it's okay," I'd cut her off. "I'm here now." The truth was, I didn't want to be reminded of all the agony I'd caused her. So we'd change the subject to the common language we understood best: beauty. I sat in one of the salon's vinyl swivel chairs and felt my mother's hands massaging dye into my thick hair, just like she used to do with amla oil before we went to mosque. She might not have approved of me going to journalism school, but we could agree on one thing: magenta would be the *perfect* colour for me.

seven

I met Abi when I was twenty-four. She was the editor of a major car company's publication that went out to dealerships across the United States, and I had applied for their editorial assistant position. I'd graduated from university the previous spring, and many of the friends I'd met in my program were struggling to find work. After completing a couple of internships at fashion magazines, I was ready for a steady gig and a regular paycheque. I had no idea what chassis or horsepower were, but I wasn't going to let that get in my way. Abi didn't seem to mind either. During the interview we mostly chatted about getting our hair cut at the same salon and how we'd both written articles for the same grassroots feminist magazine; the editorial director was also there, but it felt as though it were just Abi and me in that room, catching up like old friends. I was elated when the HR manager called me later that day to say the job was mine. (Later, Abi confessed that she'd hired me because she liked my shoes, a pair of teal flats with cut-out polka dots. "You can tell a lot about a person just by their shoes," she said. My mother used to say the same thing.)

The work itself—calling dealers in American cities I'd never heard of—was hardly thrilling, but I was happy simply to be working downtown with cool people who rode their bikes to the office and played ambient electronic music while fussing over editorial layouts. As I fact-checked sales figures, I wondered if the reps I was speaking to had ever met someone with a name like mine before. This was just a few years after 9/11, and depending on where in the U.S. I was calling, I would sometimes introduce myself as Sam. I just wanted to get on with my job without having to deal with the uneasiness in their voices or having to explain that my name is Arabic and means "tan-skinned." (My mother almost called me Sultana but thought better of it.) By that point in my life, I'd developed an M.O.: When introducing myself to a person of colour or someone with an accent, I'd say my name in Arabic, how my mother wanted it to be pronounced. To those who refuse to shorten or anglicize their name, I offer mine as an act of camaraderie. But if I'm meeting someone who looks like they've never had to correct people three times before being offered a handshake, I just accept whatever rolls off their tongues.

To ensure that the job didn't numb our creative impulses, Abi would organize fun team-building exercises: a knitting circle, a brainstorming session for our dream magazine (the one we actually wanted to work on), a trip to an auto show in Detroit so that we'd have a clue what we were writing about. She knew we had bigger hopes and dreams that didn't involve writing about car seats and winter tires. Our editorial team was different from others, made up of staff who might have ordinarily been considered a little rebellious or risky, but together we worked in perfect harmony, coming up with creative and unusual solutions to the problems we encountered—our quirks created a bond. Probably Abi had planned it that way. She cultivated a nurturing environment where a reference, no matter where it was extracted from, could be part of a larger conversation about creativity or inspiration for a story. No idea was ever shot down; every thought was valid as long as you could make a case for its boldness or relevance. Under her leadership I learned how to fight for what I believed and to let go of something when I didn't.

I was a little intimidated by how confident and self-assured Abi was, but I was also deeply fascinated by her. She had big hair, like Diana Ross at Studio 54, and conjured Bianca Jagger with her fabulous fur coat on her shoulders, a cigarette dangling from her lips. Growing up, I'd been taught that women weren't supposed to speak their minds; Abi planted the seed that as a woman in this world it's important to take up space and make yourself heard, even if it intimidates and offends powerful men. When she arrived at a conclusion before you—which she always did—she was right there with a smoke waiting for you to catch up. Her calendar was full of exciting travel plans, and she seemed to have interesting friends living unorthodox lives all across the globe.

I nursed a secret (or not-so-secret) obsession with her for months without discovering much about her personal life, though I often speculated in my head. She was so unlike any woman I'd ever encountered, and I just wanted to soak up every ounce of her fierceness. When she'd bring up how she'd eloped to Las Vegas and gotten married by Elvis, I'd see the other editors who'd been working with her for years flash her a knowing glance. One day, when Abi injured her foot, a very handsome butch named Megan came by to pick up her laptop so that she could work from home. Only then did I connect the dots—this was the person she'd married in Vegas. On top of being the coolest person I had ever met, Abi was a lesbian.

Abi was my window into a queer world I hadn't yet explored, and something told me that that was where I needed to be. It seemed much more exciting than my world at the time. In our lively conversations she'd drop references to people and topics that I'd look up online later. I'd jot down notes to myself next to scribbled nonsensical car specifications. TO RESEARCH: FAT ACTIVISM AND INGRID SISCHY. Perhaps sensing that I needed a little encouragement, Abi would provide validation when I needed it most. Once, after a string of late nights at the office, she gathered the entire editorial team to present me with a certificate she'd had the art department create in the midst of looming deadlines. It looked like a diploma and read, THE FUTURE IS HERE BUT THERE IS SO MUCH MORE TO COME! I was so touched by the gesture that I cried in the bathroom.

There are many ways to come out. Sometimes the label comes first. Sometimes it's through action or experience. Some people say they've always known, and for others the process of realization is gradual. It might not be a single big moment but rather an accumulation of little ones. By my mid-twenties, I decided to try on the label of queer to see how it fit. I would casually allude to being queer in conversations with my friends and my siblings. I carefully studied their faces and body language for any hint of surprise or discomfort. If I was with friends and we spotted two women—especially two femmes—making out on a dance floor, I'd be the recipient of a knowing glance. Or we'd be sitting in a park, discreetly drinking prosecco out of plastic cups, and Andrew would tell me I was the prettiest lesbian he knew. It made me smile to know that I was seen even if I was still partly in hiding.

It was Andrew who'd taken me to my first queer party, where I watched him flirt with a boy who, we discovered—to our delight—had lesbian moms. By the end of the night they'd made out for so long they were awarded a prize. It was the first time I'd seen Andrew kiss a boy, and he seemed so free, so himself. I felt a vague urge to make out with some of the girls at the party, but I wasn't ready to act upon it. Instead I dodged eye contact, making my way to a different part of the dance floor if I felt their eyes on me for a few seconds too long. Although I was coming to terms with my attraction to women—which had started with my childhood infatuation with Sonia and followed me into the change rooms of my adolescence—I still felt I owed it to Peter to at least be faithful, if nothing else. Peter was always overworked and largely absent from my life; I wondered if the only reason we were still together was that I rarely saw him. Friends at school and work took to calling me "the married single woman" and joked about whether Peter actually existed. I felt I was living a lie.

When Andrew started dating Philip, a clothing designer, I saw even more new opportunities open up to me. He and Philip were going to New York for a show that featured emerging designers, filmmakers, and visual artists. Philip was presenting his new menswear collection to media and buyers, and Andrew invited me to join them, convinced that New York City was a place I simply had to experience for myself. I hadn't left the country since my family had arrived from Pakistan more than fifteen years before, but I gathered my nerve and booked my ticket. I crashed on the couch in the loft they'd rented in Chelsea, and together we ran through the sequence of runway looks as we'd done in the past for Philip's shows in Toronto, when friends would pitch in curating the music, photographing the outfits, and sewing at the studio. We were all eager to imagine new ways to challenge ourselves creatively while also recognizing how special it was to have friends who always wanted to do more. Thanks to Andrew, who had a knack for sensing people's strengths, we'd found one another. On the floor of the loft, the three of us laid out shots of each outfit and moved them around like chess pieces: plaid garments with hits of blue and green first, followed by solid blues and greens providing continuity from the plaid, and then a tweed coat with a striking fur collar (the pièce de résistance) to finish things off with high drama.

The day after the show, we did what anyone with an afternoon to kill in Manhattan would do: we went shopping. In a department store on West 34th Street, Philip eyed a leather motorcycle jacket across the room that he thought was "very Samra"—a more feminine version of the men's jackets I would try on at his studio that were always a little too big on me. I abandoned the rack of jumpers I was perusing and tried it on. The jacket fit perfectly, as though it had been tailored specifically for my body—it was meant to be. I stared at this new version of myself in the mirror. Once again, my friends had seen me before I saw myself.

Through Philip I began to meet many new queer men and women. It was at a New Year's Eve party thrown by one of Philip's architect friends that I came upon Kristina. She had a reddish-bronze Louise Brooks bob and eyes that gleamed like an icy lake. From across the room I watched her tinker with the string of lights coiling around the Christmas tree. There was a selective aloofness about Kristina that drew me in: she seemed altogether unaware of the fight that had broken out between two drugged-out partygoers in the hallway as she meticulously adjusted the decorations adorning the tree. I used the coincidence of our wearing the same outfit—identical vests and skinny jeans—as an icebreaker. I had a sudden compulsion to brush my hand against her cheek, but I restrained myself. Once the tree was set up to her satisfaction, we went up to the roof to share a cigarette. Kristina stood with a hand supporting her elbow, the light from the ember casting an orange glow on her skin. When it got windy, her hair would sweep across her face and stick to the gloss on her lips. As the smoking filled the silence between us, she stared at me and took a long drag, as if to ask, "Now what?" The electricity between us was strong enough that friends who came over to join our conversation would just as quickly leave, as though they'd walked in on someone undressing. A girl took a Polaroid of us and wrote VEST FRIENDS FOREVER on it in black Sharpie. I wanted to taste Kristina's lip balm, to gently tuck her hair behind her ear. Instead I watched the other queer couples make out after the countdown, intensely aware of my own loneliness.

I arrived home that night to find Peter passed out on the couch with a bloody nose. After his shift at the restaurant (and one too many New Year's toasts), he'd drunkenly fallen on the pavement while walking home. Our separate— and very different—evenings reminded me how far we'd drifted from each other. Our relationship, which at the best of times had felt platonic, now felt like an obstacle to our happiness. I was living with a roommate I had nothing in common with. And I had changed: I barely resembled my former self, the version of me who sought acceptance and security—or was it invisibility?—in a heterosexual marriage.

In the new year we started going to couple's counselling and acknowledged to the therapist that the reason we felt we were growing distant was that we weren't moving forward as a couple. Peter said he felt undesired in the relationship because I never wanted to have sex with him. When the therapist asked me why that was, I couldn't find the courage to say that I wanted to be with women. That it wasn't that I was asexual, as I had suspected for so long—it was that I was denying myself the freedom to be the person I longed to be.

That year, I spent Eid with my family. Eid was the only Muslim holiday I observed at that point in my life, and one of the few times a year I saw my father. I'd started visiting again in my late twenties, partly out of guilt—I felt I had to spend Eid with my parents, and my mom would be disappointed if I didn't show. By then she'd sold her salon, at my father's urging, so there were fewer opportunities for us to connect. There was still tension between us all, so the atmosphere was far from celebratory. My father would order us lunch from his favourite Pakistani restaurant and present us with Eid money, and then drive me home. This particular year was memorable, though, because during the car ride he apologized for the cruelty I'd endured from him as a child. I was shocked. I'd never heard my dad apologize in his entire life; everything was always our fault. He offered to help Peter and me buy a place so that we could move out of our shabby rental apartment. By then I'd left my job at the car company and was working at an advertising agency— maybe it was, after all, time for an upgrade. So in lieu of filing for divorce, Peter and I bought a condo. We thought that deciding on the right shade of charcoal for the walls and the perfect height for bar stools would rescue our sinking marriage. We were working toward a common goal.

In the end, the move only heightened the fact that couple's therapy and paint chips couldn't fix what had been broken for so long. A few months after we bought the condo, despair set in. The shame I carried with me, and the burden of hiding my authentic self, was almost too much for me to bear—once again I entertained thoughts of suicide. I called a crisis centre one night. The next day, as I oversaw a beauty shoot for a major client, managing a team of photographers, stylists, models, and hair and makeup artists, I got a call from the centre, making sure I hadn't killed myself. I excused myself, hid in the bathroom, and cried before returning to the set to check that the models' hair was just the right amount of wavy.

It was my father who called it. I was over at my parents' for a visit and said that I couldn't stay for dinner, Peter and I had plans. My father, with uncharacteristic intimacy, lowered his voice and asked me if I was thinking about ending my marriage. I was thrown off by his intuition and sat silent for a moment, staring at the face that looked so much like my own. In that moment, I recognized that I was a part of him. My eyes welled up as he wrapped his arms around me. He held me for as long as I needed to be held. As his white cotton sleeves absorbed my tears and I rested my head on his chest, I was reminded of how comforting I had found his body odour as a child.

Finally, I told my parents that I was not happy in my marriage and yes, I wanted to end it. Saying it out loud, at last, made it real. They didn't ask me to explain myself. Instead of unpacking what exactly had gone wrong or sorting through my complicated emotions, my father laid out the practical steps I needed to take to sell our condo, providing me with names of real estate agents and lawyers. His focus on the logistics was its own kind of support—the only kind he knew how to give. I wanted to tell him how much the distance between us had hurt me over the years, and how I believed that his failure to parent me was partly what had led to my relationship with Peter in the first place. But I understood that my need for closure with my father was a product of the culture I grew up in that placed so much emphasis on it. He didn't have the tools to understand the psychological impact his parenting had on my life—I couldn't expect him to acknowledge his wrongdoings. So I let him reclaim his parental role in his own particular fashion. Closure, for me, would mean accepting my circumstances rather than trying to alter them to serve me best.

That evening, as I travelled home on the subway, I practised how I would deliver the news to Peter. I turned up Depeche Mode on my headphones so loud I was sure my eardrums would rupture. My footsteps got heavier as I entered our building and passed the concierge who always called me Ms. Habib. (I love being called by my last name, which means "beloved" in Arabic—it reminds me that I am worthy of love.) When I opened the door, Peter was preparing to roast a chicken for us for dinner. I could smell the roasted potatoes that were already in the oven after being deep-fried, a recipe he'd adapted from his South African grandmother, who had welcomed me with open arms when I was estranged from my own family.

I lingered at the door for a minute, taking in the illusion of domestic bliss. "We need to talk," I told him.

Perhaps sensing what I was about to say, Peter took longer than usual to season the chicken while I waited on the balcony with a glass of wine. When he finally came out to join me, his body seemed to already carry the weight of heartbreak. I couldn't say why Peter had chosen to stay with me for this long, but one thing I was certain of: we both deserved so much more. There was no use drawing it out, so I got straight to the point. Afterwards we cried for hours on our little balcony, cars zipping by on the highway below as if nothing was out of the ordinary.

eight

I stuffed the semi-deflated air mattress into the closet and tidied the counters and tabletops to achieve the preferred level of staging. Artificial flowers: *check*. Ikea candles: *check*. Peter and I had sold our condo, and until my new apartment came available in another month, I was staying in a condo my parents had bought for themselves and just as quickly put up for sale. They had thought that living in a small space downtown would be easier than maintaining their large empty house in the suburbs, which filled up only during the holidays, when my sisters visited from New York, where they were both working, one as a documentary filmmaker and the other as a lawyer. But they quickly discovered that condo living wasn't conducive to social interaction, and they moved back home to be close to their mosque. The only lasting connections they'd built in Canada were with other Pakistanis from the Ahmadiyya community. Together they could pretend they'd never left home—they'd built a mini Rabwah of their own in a suburb of Toronto. My father was so desperate to get rid of the condo that he dropped the asking price a little bit more every day.

I was putting in long hours at the ad agency, where staying at the office till midnight to meet client deadlines was an accepted part of the job. I'd been unhappy in my marriage for so long that working late had become a welcome distraction—the longer I stayed at the office, writing taglines for alcohol and tampon ads, the less time I'd have for facing my crumbling marriage. But now that I'd left Peter my world felt cracked wide open, and I decided to do something I'd been thinking about for a long time but had always been too afraid to follow through with: I booked a trip to Japan.

My curiosity had been sparked in ESL class, back when I'd hide out in the library reading books about Japan to escape my bullies, buoyed by the fact that I shared a home continent with Ms. Nakamura. Since then, I perked up any time Japan was mentioned, whether I was reading a Haruki Murakami novel or an indie blog about avant-garde architecture. I was itching to experience it first-hand. I found other friends who were just as obsessed as I was, and we forwarded each other links to beautiful onsens and modern museums located on forested hills.

Aside from my jaunt to New York, I hadn't left Canada in my adult life. I'd certainly never travelled alone before. I used to roll my eyes at people who went on trips to "find themselves." *You're right here! What is there to find?* I'd say to myself as friends took off to Barcelona or Paris to get a fresh perspective and experience a different pace of life. My sisters, who'd lived and worked in different countries, would send me links to the exciting places they'd visited (*I liked Palais de Tokyo but you'd LOVE it!* or, *Samra, you absolutely HAVE to see the Blue Mosque*), trying to chip away at the fear that had held me back all these years. Sometimes they were blunt and told me I needed to leave my comfort zone and see the world. I'd been on autopilot for so long, pretending I was fine with the way things were. Instead of shaking things up and risking uncertainty—a feeling I'd been running from ever since childhood—I convinced myself that I didn't need the things that brought others closer to self-awareness. In truth, I had been afraid of who I might find and of realizing what I had denied myself. Now I understood that there was a whole world I'd been hiding from, and I was finally ready to discover it.

As I scoured the Airbnb listings for Tokyo, I came across a room in an apartment in Shinjuku with the headline CENTRAL, GAY-FRIENDLY, AND CLEAN. The avatar next to the listing showed a black man with a generous smile. The prospect of my host in this foreign land being gay—or at least gay-friendly—instantly put me at ease. I contacted the owner, Loren, and introduced myself, saying I was also interested in visiting Kyoto and casually mentioning that I too was queer—realizing as I typed them that I'd never written those words before. I stared at the screen for a few minutes, the cursor blinking in sync with my heartbeat, before hitting SEND.

Loren wrote back a detailed message with everything I needed to know (and things I hadn't even considered). And he promised to take me to queer bars in Tokyo. I picked up my BlackBerry and typed a message to Abi: *I'm not going to be afraid anymore.*

In the years since she'd been my boss, Abi had become a mentor and a close friend. As I came to know her and Megan better outside of work, our friendship evolved and intensified—I even nicknamed them "my lesbian moms." I could always depend on them, for everything from middle-of-the-night relationship advice to congratulatory voicemails from whatever part of the world they happened to be in. (Instead of buying a house and having children like all the other couples I knew, they spent their money on stints in Berlin and Mexico and investing in art, often by queer artists.) They lent me books with their insightful notes scribbled in the margins, and they always listened to my problems with an open mind, offering encouragement when my faith in myself dwindled.

Most important, in Abi and Megan I saw an example of how I could live my life differently from what I'd been told, and an example of what a queer relationship could look like for me. Before I met them, love had felt suffocating, a chore, something you had to give up your freedom for.

Theirs was a true partnership, in which they supported each other in ways I had never witnessed growing up. Through observing them, I realized I didn't have to pursue a "conventional" life. My aspirations didn't have to be to get married and have children; finding myself through exploring the unknown was a much more worthy ambition.

"You'll be surprised by the version of yourself you'll meet when you travel," Megan would say.

I was about to find out.

After I'd checked in at the airport and exchanged my money into yen, it struck me that no one in my family knew I was about to travel halfway across the globe. When I had told my parents I was leaving Peter, my mother assumed I'd move back home and live with them. *Finally she's come to her senses!* How could I resist their undivided attention and hospitality for the rest of my life? I was so used to keeping my life a secret from my parents that telling them about my plans hadn't occurred to me. We'd been estranged for so long I wondered if I'd ever even shared my love for Japan with them. I looked around for a pay phone.

"Hi, Mom. I'm at the airport about to board a plane to Japan. I just thought I'd call you and tell you that." I eyed an apple strudel at the coffee shop.

By this point in her life my mother had seen and heard it all; she was immune to shock. In the years since I'd run away from home, my parents' feelings about my disastrous arranged marriage had crystallized into guilt. They felt I'd been through enough and didn't owe them an explanation for how I chose to live my life. Now, they genuinely just wanted me to be happy.

The only thing my mother asked was if I was travelling with a lover, or if I was meeting a lover in Japan. I told her I was alone, but I didn't dare add that I'd be staying with a man who promised to show me the queer nightlife in Tokyo. We said goodbye, and I told her I loved her.

Every sound seemed to be happening at a distance, as if too courteous to disrupt my inner thoughts: the slow and gentle swoosh of cars driving over puddles of rain, as if saying *Pardon me, but it won't be too loud, it'll be over in a second,* the gentle closing of doors, as if trying not to wake a newborn baby. Even the breeze after the rain felt subtle against my skin, warming up to the idea of me. Perhaps that's why people travel, to see the mechanics of everyday life from a different angle. I'd stayed still for so long—what else had I been missing?

I felt like I was in a Godard film as I followed the looping uphill path to Loren's apartment in a state of suspended quiet, the only dialogue in my head. Loren buzzed me up, and when he came to the door he welcomed me with such warmth and familiarity that I felt I was reuniting with an old friend.

"Wow, you're beautiful!" he said, grabbing my luggage and leading me to my room. His partner had extended a business trip in Spain, so it would just be the two of us. A Harvard grad, Loren had worked in business development for various media companies before making Japan his home. Like me, he'd always been intrigued by Japanese culture, but unlike me, he'd fuelled his passion by learning the language while still living in America.

"Girl, we're going dancing!" he announced. I tried to explain how tired I was, given the time difference and the fact that I'd spent the entire flight next to a teething baby. But Loren wasn't interested in my excuses: we were going to Ni-chōme, Tokyo's gay district, and that was that. He disappeared into his room and came back in a fresh outfit: fitted grey jeans and a black muscle T with YES WE CAN emblazoned across the chest. I changed into the leather motorcycle jacket and black jeans that had become my uniform of late.

At the bar in Ni-chōme I ordered a beer and joined Loren and two of his friends outside for a cigarette. Both were fit white men in their twenties who were teaching English in Tokyo's suburbs while figuring out what they wanted to do with their lives. We smoked and shared stories of what had led us here. I looked up at the dark sky diluted by the lights of nighttime Tokyo: it was hard to believe that just twenty-four hours ago I was at my desk in Toronto eating a salad.

After finishing a round of beers, we moved on to a gay dance club just a few steps away. I broke off from the group and made my way to the bar to order a drink. As I weaved through the crowd, I noticed a man who could very well have been my cousin drinking at a table by himself. We acknowledged each other, the only two brown people in a gay bar in Tokyo. His smile felt like an invitation to say hi, so I introduced myself. Hassan, whose parents were from Pakistan, had lived in different parts of Asia throughout his life. Beijing was now his home, but he travelled often for work. He was in Tokyo to shoot a food documentary for a TV network. We briefly spoke in Urdu after he asked me what brought me to Japan. It was surreal to be in a gay bar in Tokyo speaking in my native tongue with a gay Pakistani man from Beijing—like finding a missing puzzle piece under the coffee table while spring cleaning. I wondered where I'd find the rest of the pieces. Although we were both visitors, the interaction made me feel for a moment as though that club and Tokyo were home—as if I'd always been there. Maybe home was simply any place where you felt seen and welcome. Hassan's eyes twinkled when a tall man approached; I said goodbye and continued on to the bar.

I became acutely aware that I was the only woman in the place as I attempted to get the bartender's attention. Even though the tall Asian man next to me had been waiting longer, he nudged me to let me know I could order first. When the bartender returned with our orders, we clinked our beer bottles together. Felix was visiting from Taiwan for the weekend, and lamented that a boy he'd been flirting with online for a few months was now ignoring his texts.

"You have really big breasts," he said.

Thrown by his non sequitur, I tugged on the front of my jacket to cover my chest. "Thanks," I said. "I guess."

"Are you into men or women?" he asked bluntly, studying my face and body.

"I . . . I'm queer," I said.

It was the first time I'd said the words aloud. I'd said that I liked girls, and that I wanted to be with girls, but this was a new milestone. Perhaps by wearing the armour of anonymity in a city that wasn't mine, I could speak them without caring about the consequences.

"What does that mean? Like, who are you into?" Felix asked. His questions were starting to feel invasive, and I wished he'd go back to being sad about his online boyfriend.

"I guess I'm . . . I'm attracted to everyone, but I'm mostly into women." I felt like I was sorting through my entire identity in one throwaway conversation.

"I've always wanted to know," he began. "How do you have sex with women?"

My body tensed. I didn't have the courage to admit that I'd never actually had sex with a woman before. "It's . . . you know, fun. It's great. Listen, my friend is probably wondering where I am," I said, and started to move away.

"Hey, the girl bar is across the street, if you were wondering. And you have to check out the Harajuku district. There's really great shopping there. Nice to meet you, Samra!"

I wasn't quite ready for the girl bar yet. I was still processing the fact that I'd just come out to a stranger. I hurried off, as though recovering from a fall I hoped nobody had witnessed.

I went to Harajuku the very next day. Loren drew a detailed map with helpful instructions for each place I might want to visit: museums, galleries, architectural marvels. I avoided the large crowds in touristy areas and instead strolled along quiet alleyways, popping my earbuds in to create my own soundtrack. I walked by tiny houses with miniature gardens efficiently packed with a wealth of plants and wondered how I'd fill my new apartment back home. What would the new me find absolutely necessary to live with, and what could she do without? It was hard to imagine a space that was solely for my joy and comfort and no one else's. Did I even know how to live a life that put me first? I felt a sudden longing, but I didn't know for whom or for what. It wasn't for Peter or my parents. I let myself dwell in the feeling instead of shoving it away.

And then I realized that it was fear—fear that no one would ever truly understand me and love every part of me. The only relationships I'd ever known felt like bargaining and settling: bargaining for space to be free, settling for a partner who didn't wonder what I was up to. I wanted someone to see all of me, the good and the bad. I was in such a rush to prove that I'd come out of childhood un-scathed, in order to prevent causing others any worry and concern, that I'd forgotten to examine whether I truly had. The realization was so startling that I sat down on a bench and cried. Two Japanese punks with bleached-blond hair and dressed entirely in black stood outside a streetwear shop, smoking and studying me. One walked up and gave me a flyer to a gallery opening later that night.

I came across a French clothing boutique run by two young Japanese kids. Past the oversized smocks and jackets I spotted a silk dress with painted leaves in oranges, golds, and greens. I tried it on and felt how tightly it hugged my body. I had shied away from clothes that showed off my curves, opting instead to drown in oversized sweaters and baggy dresses. Ironically, after having prayed for curves in my youth, I spent my twenties feeling self-conscious about my hips, concealing them in pants that were several sizes too large.

In the mirror, I adjusted my posture and examined my body. Maybe being a woman could be a source of power for me. What would it feel like to walk through the world daring to present myself without apology? Why had I never given myself permission to marvel at my body and appreciate how resilient it had been? How it had gently carried me through pain and trauma, and how for years I hid it under layers of shame. Because my femininity had often been exploited by others, used as justification for controlling and monitoring me, I didn't want it to be looked at or acknowledged. Now, looking at myself as if for the first time, I understood how showing off my curves could allow me to take back the power from those who had stripped me of it. My body could be a source of joy and pride. It was for me and for me alone. Determined to find out what enjoying it could feel like, I handed the cashier my credit card and made my only purchase in Japan. I wondered if Andrew and Philip would call it "very Samra" when I wore it to their upcoming wedding.

After Tokyo, I took the train to a tiny guest house in Kyoto, where I spent the rest of my trip. I rented a bicycle and zipped around the city to imprint its every corner onto my memory. I watched with delight as people of all ages—from toddlers to octogenarians—wandered through the Manga Museum and sat reading comics on the surrounding astroturf. Seeing them all getting enjoyment from the same source made me wonder: why don't we ever see someone above the age of fifty being pushed on the swings or eating an ice cream cone with sprinkles?

For the rest of my trip, I let my instincts guide me. When I reached the top of a hill on my search for a particular temple, I smelled a warm and familiar scent. Instead of following the stairs, I used the smoky smell as my map and made a detour to my left, where I came across a crowd of people gathered around a large incense burner, purifying themselves before entering the temple. The smell of sandalwood reminded me of my mother, who used to burn sticks of it in Pakistan to prepare our house for guests. No matter how far away I went, I always came back to her.

I walked farther east and came across gardens that were protected by majestic wooden gates. The elegant building beyond them seemed off-limits, like rare and expensive pottery kept behind a locked glass door in a shop. Was there a family inside having a meal? I wondered. Were there children playing in the garden under the cherry blossoms? The guard, perhaps sensing my curiosity, smiled and unlocked the door. Even though we spoke different languages, we understood each other. Hesitant at first,

I walked a narrow path that led me to a cemetery, where I saw row upon row of neatly staggered tombstones. It was meticulously landscaped, with hardly a stray leaf or pebble in sight. Here, too, the air was perfumed with sandalwood incense from the nearby temple. I considered the vast sky above the elaborate tombstones, framed as it was by cherry blossoms and maple trees, and marvelled at life, at the lightness that comes from unburdening oneself of a secret. How far I'd travelled to arrive at a simple truth about myself. I closed my eyes and listened to the rock doves cooing in the distance.

I was ready to go home. I was ready to find my people.

nine

Back in Toronto, I began to explore another new frontier: online dating. As I set about the task of filling out my profile, portioning my identity into a series of designated fields, I was confronted with the obvious question: was I interested in men or in women? I stared at my monitor for what felt like an eternity. I still didn't have the courage to go on a date with a woman, even though I really wanted to. How did women flirt with other women? What if I did it wrong?

Delaying the inevitable, I took the easy route. And so I met Alex, who was tall and slim with a mop of curly hair. His eyes were the blue of a saltbox house in the Maritimes. And he'd slept with more men than I had (not a high bar to clear), which made him seem like a safe option. He'd also been in polyamorous relationships, and many of the women he'd dated identified as queer. I was intrigued.

Alex was the kind of cool, handsome boyfriend that made parents (never mind strict Muslim parents) nervous, but with a twist. He wasn't interested in committing to a singular gender expression. For him, every day was a new opportunity to challenge people's perceptions around masculinity. It was disarming to hear him say "Listen, sister!" and grab the nail polish from my hands, certain he could do a better job painting my fingernails. He'd acted in some short films in his twenties, and I remember the thrill I felt watching him perform drag onscreen, with a blond wig and smudged red lipstick. I was transfixed; he looked so pretty, so hauntingly himself.

He was nothing like the men I'd known growing up—men I was terrified of. I listened spellbound to his stories of living in New York in the nineties, waiting tables at Veselka in the East Village in his twenties, almost being kidnapped while looking for drugs in Morocco, hitchhiking through eastern Europe with barely a penny to his name. Granted, he was eleven years older than me, but he'd lived so much, whereas I felt I hadn't lived at all. Alex was my crash course in a life I'd missed out on. He was complicated, but his voracious appetite for experience stirred a storm inside me. Together, we were never bored. We listened to music by Bauhaus, PJ Harvey, and Liz Phair, and because of him I started paying attention to the meanings behind the songs instead of just the beats that compelled me to dance. I discovered that many of my favourite songs sampled older, better songs. That my favourite writers were inspired by older, better writers. With Alex, I inched closer to finding my place in the world.

We agreed that we would date and sleep with other people. (I remember thinking to myself, *Samra, you've really come a long way,* as I watched my boyfriend make out with a man on the dance floor at a queer party.) I still craved the comfort of being in a relationship, but I wanted to experience being with women and femmes. My relationship with Alex was my armour, a convenient setup for someone who was trying to imagine what being queer looked like and was terrified.

Together, we travelled all over. My stamp-covered passport told the story of our relationship and of all the ways I discovered myself in it. There was Berlin, where I went to my first sex club, and the bouncer politely asked me if I would pee in a cup for him because that was his kink, and inside I met a dominatrix who paid for school by selling her eggs to a gay Asian American couple. There was Istanbul, where we spent some time with queers who were fed up with the violence many faced under Erdoğan's shadow and, after watching one of the only lesbian bars get shut down, wanted to build a commune outside the city. I probably wouldn't have felt safe visiting these places had I not been swept along by Alex's restless sense of adventure. Visiting different parts of myself in those spaces made me love myself, my body, and my life even more.

And then there was Montreal, where we met Tiffany at a bar that smelled of stale cigarette smoke. The carpet on the patio looked as though it hadn't been cleaned in decades. Tiffany had buzzed blond hair and bleached eyebrows that made her look like a femme fatale in a sci-fi film. When I kissed her hello on the cheeks, I smelled a mix of patchouli and rose oil on her. Rose always reminded me of Pakistan; I lingered a few seconds too long. She wore a large fur coat to protect against the harsh Montreal winter and black steel-toed boots that made her look like she was ready for battle. When we took her back to our rented apartment, she told us about the punk band she played with. I watched the beginnings of intimacy between Alex and Tiffany. Even spontaneous erotic moments can seem so measured and calculated, like a waltz: you know exactly what's coming. The laptop lit up their faces as they watched Tiffany's band perform at a dingy bar in a small town. Alex pretended to like it and asked to see more; his interest thrilled Tiffany. With each video her fingers lingered on his shoulders a bit longer. I glanced out the window at the gentle flurries that had begun. *Tiffany will have one hell of a walk home*, I thought. *Good thing she wore those boots.*

I scrolled through my iPod and settled on Stereolab, lit a cigarette from Alex's pack and smoked on the leather couch facing Alex and Tiffany. I watched them continue to lay the groundwork. Tiffany rested her head on Alex's shoulder as he played with the back of her neck. I did a quick gut check and determined that I didn't feel even the slightest pang of jealousy as my boyfriend kissed the girl we'd picked up just an hour ago. He was a beautiful kisser—why hadn't I noticed that before? His hands framing her face, the wrinkle of his mouth, his eyelashes brushing against her skin: I was seeing Alex the lover, not Alex my boyfriend. He was so tender and familiar with her. Suddenly Tiffany stopped kissing Alex and turned to me with a smirk, offering me her hand. She laughed easily. She called out my name in her thick Québécois accent, mangling it slightly. But there was no point disrupting our encounter with the tedious process of correction (and she'd signed up for a threesome, not an Arabic lesson). We would never see each other again. I could have been Leila, Ayesha, or Fatima that night.

I stubbed my cigarette in the ashtray and walked toward her, gave her my hand and rested the other on her waist. She wore a white silk slip under her mohair sweater. I felt her round ass as she grabbed mine through my jeans. For a few moments, we almost slow danced; Tiffany's hips swayed to the song, and I traced my hands down her hourglass figure. I touched the back of her shaved head and felt the prickly new growth of hair. I stared at her lips and asked her if it was okay to kiss her. I felt her hot whisky breath on me as I teased her chapped bottom lip with mine.

When it was over, the three of us shared a cigarette in bed and talked about our plans for the rest of the weekend. I confessed to Tiffany that she was the first girl I'd ever had sex with. She stared at me for a moment before kissing me on the lips, the smell of tobacco on her skin.

My relationship with Alex was perfect, until I'd learned everything it could possibly teach me. I learned what fluidity looked like, and how to enjoy my body with a spectrum of queer lovers. And through it all Alex provided an anchor, which I will be forever grateful for. My vision of what being queer looked like was coming into focus.

But I couldn't help feeling that being with Alex, a cis man, was my way of continuing to hide. I had hidden myself for so long, ever since Khola denied having seen me at the Ahmadi mosque. I had internalized the message that hiding would protect me, but I didn't realize the dangerous pattern this created. My relationship with Alex felt like another cloak, affording me the opportunity to be with queer people in private without fear of judgment or repercussions. But my fears were leftovers from a past that I had moved beyond, and I was tired of hiding.

I knew it was time to pursue relationships with women and people who identified as trans and non-binary. I wanted to hold their hands and kiss in public, two people whom society rejected, dismissed, and disapproved of daring to be seen, daring to be in love even when we were told we weren't allowed to be. I wouldn't let the fact that I was coming out of a relationship with a man make me feel that I wasn't queer enough—being queer, I learned, is so much more than who you sleep with. It's who you are, whether that means rejecting traditional gender roles or embracing non-normative identities and politics.

After Alex, my love life continued to be shaped by travel and online dating. In my twenties, my view of the world had been exceptionally small—I relied heavily on imagination to fill in the gaps in my limited knowledge. Now, not only were my romantic encounters catalysts to self-awareness, but they were also informing my experience of how race and desire intersect. As a person of colour travelling without a partner, I was opening myself up to a whole new host of lessons.

The dating apps on my phone became a gauge for where I was desired and where I was not. In Berlin, where even a hint of a tan is considered highly desirable, my phone is bombarded with messages, mostly from white German lesbians who are starved for colour. In Paris, which suffers from a dearth of queer people of colour on dating apps, I resort to having a late-night drink with a friendly man who is never white. I figure that a conversation with an interesting person who has a different perspective on the city I'm visiting is better than staying in my Airbnb all night. In Sweden, I get so few messages that I have to restart my phone to make sure it's working.

Throughout my travels, I thought about what I wanted love to look like for me. Was it possible to be loved without losing myself? Was the absence of a partner I was spiritually and intellectually in sync with the price I had to pay for being uncompromising about needing the space to grow?

Once, while staying with a friend at a little-known queer haven in Mexico, I was on the beach watching my friend surf when three Mexican women approached and asked if they could join me. Travelling to unknown places had sharpened my intuition, and something told me I could trust these women. As the sun began to set, one of them lit a stick of palo santo, and she and I talked about the feeling of falling in love: how it made us cautious, how we were both suspicious of any feeling that's unpredictable and causes us to lose control. As we compared our Virgo traits, we learned that we had the exact same birthday. The discovery made us laugh. Dusk descended, and the women invited me to celebrate the new moon with them in a nearby mountain town. Not wanting to miss out on this one-of-a-kind experience, I didn't think twice about hitching a ride with a group of construction workers on their way to a job, sitting in the flatbed with some of the men and their equipment. They dropped me off in the town, where the Mexican elders (who I suspected were a lesbian couple) had gathered with a dozen other women and femmes around my age. We talked about how not to lose oneself while giving and receiving love and how to keep our sense of self intact while opening ourselves up to the possibility of love. I marvelled at the sheer longevity of this battle, how it united us across age and geography.

In the spring of 2015, almost two decades after my rushed wedding to Nasir, I watched my sister marry her husband in a beautiful ceremony at the Aga Khan Museum in Toronto. Needless to say, it was a much more joyful affair than my own. My sister walked down the aisle to a Hindi song my relatives had sung at my parents' wedding. The lovely homage to them, reimagined by cellists, sent shivers down my spine. Suddenly the uneasiness I felt around the idea of weddings, rooted in the trauma I carried with me from being arranged to marry at such a young age, seemed to melt away. One by one, friends took the podium and delivered heartfelt speeches about the bride and groom. There were friends they'd met in law school, friends made while studying at Oxford, Americans who'd journeyed north of the border for the occasion. It was clear how much they loved my sister, and I listened, rapt, as they described an entirely different version of her from the one I grew up with. I was being introduced to a remarkable new person.

I couldn't help wondering if such declarations of love required the exchanging of vows as a backdrop. What if I were to renew my vows to myself, and ask guests to share what our friendship means to them? Did I need the occasion of marriage to feel validated by those I love, or to celebrate love itself?

I started to think about the incredible, lasting friendships I'd made over the years—with Andrew, with Abi and Megan. Maybe my friends—my chosen family—could be the loves of my life. After all, chosen families are a cornerstone of queer culture, especially for those whose biological families don't accept them. As we grow into ourselves, we amass a network of friends who embrace us as we are and nurture us in ways we never were while growing up. My friends, my soul mates, see all of me—the messy and the tender parts. They know what needs to be celebrated and what still needs healing.

I wasn't going to have another wedding, I was sure. (In some ways, I felt I was living my life backwards: I got marriage out of my system when I was still a kid, and now I was carefree and untethered.) My friends wouldn't have a platform to deliver a poignant speech about how we met, but they could show me how much they cared in other ways:

checking in during their coffee breaks when I'm upset over a racist encounter, surreptitiously leaving a Polaroid of a moody Halifax sunset on my desk because it reminds them of me, an invitation to go for a quiet walk on the beach or simply to sit in the kitchen with them while they bake an apple pie because there's a whisper of fall in the air. Being surrounded by great people isn't a fluke. It's almost like solving a math problem, finding variables, adding and subtracting to figure out a formula that works. Being surrounded by people who fuel you is intentional.

"Leave young people in a better state than you found them in," a friend once told me. The advice had been passed on by her father (who, it happened, was significantly older than his wife). I couldn't help thinking about this line as it applied to Shireen. Shireen was the youngest person I'd ever slept with. A gender nonconformist, they had settled on *they* as the pronoun that fit best, like the tight hijab they wore while skateboarding through our neighbourhood. Shireen had lied to me about their age, letting me believe they were in their twenties when in fact they were nineteen.

Being with Shireen was like sleeping with a younger version of myself. They were Iranian and had the same hunger for life and experience that their upbringing had deprived them of. After finding out their real age, we decided it was best for us to shift our dynamic. We both recognized that what we'd stumbled upon was bigger than just a casual hookup. I would have them over and cook elaborate "family" dinners. "It smells like home!" they would say, breathing in the spices and removing their hijab to reveal the hair colour of the week: orange, hot pink, acid green. Their parents, who had left Iran to escape the oppressive grip of Islamic governance, didn't understand why Shireen would choose to wear the hijab. There was no place in Islam for people who skateboarded around in short skirts, showing off their hairy legs. But Shireen looked like the queer Iranian action figure *I* would have wanted, if such a thing existed. They seemed to have made a mission out of proving there was no one way to be Muslim.

Shireen would come over and read Persian poetry to me while I played with their hair and checked if it needed extra conditioning. They would untangle the knots in mine as I gave a detailed account of my latest breakup and what kind of art the experience inspired me to create. ("Like a giant black parachute trapped in a tiny room," I would explain. "Suffocating.") Shireen would nod understandingly and sketch what I'd been describing. They would point out words that were similar to Persian when we listened to old Urdu songs my father used to play while braiding my hair for school. Slowly, we were shifting into a parent-child dynamic that neither of us had anticipated. But it felt right. We both instinctively knew there was a reason our paths had crossed. I liked to imagine that Shireen was my younger self coming back into my life for a second chance. *Tell them what you needed to hear at their age*, I'd say to myself as they described the same problems I was having when I was in my early twenties.

And so I'd repeat the wisdom of my lesbian moms, which had once helped put me back together: "You have everything you need. I can't wait for people to see what I've known all along—that you're amazing."

ten

The email landed in my inbox just before Christmas. I'd been anticipating its arrival for days. Every time my phone lit up, my stomach would tighten and my heart would start pounding. Call it intuition, a gut feeling, but even then I knew that a response would change everything.

"Do you want to join us this Friday? 1:10–2:30."

I had contacted El-Farouk Khaki, the co-founder of Unity Mosque, after hearing about a prayer space that welcomed queer Muslims. Khaki, an openly gay human rights lawyer who fled Tanzania in the 1970s, founded the mosque in 2009 with his husband, Troy Jackson, a Muslim convert. Mosques that are run by queer imams and welcome queer Muslims are not advertised on public forums or on social media. If you don't happen to know someone who attends one, it's almost impossible to know they exist, and for good reason: safety is a major concern for attendees. Many are refugees who've fled Muslim countries where being gay is still punishable by death.

I hadn't set foot inside a mosque since my late teens, when I broke my *nikah* and dissolved my marriage to Nasir. I'd been swiftly shunned by the mosque aunties, who, taking on the role of spokespersons for Islam, ruled that my actions made me a Bad Muslim. Suddenly there was no place for me in that sacred place of worship that had once been a source of comfort and stability. Worried I'd be a bad influence on their daughters, the aunties watched my friends like hawks to ensure that none of them would so much as respond to my "Assalam-o-Alaikum" greeting. Worst of all, they made my mother feel as though she'd done a bad job raising me. My rebellion had been a direct challenge to that central tenet of Muslim households: parents and elders know best.

When we moved to Canada, the mosque had been my mother's refuge, a place where she wasn't judged on how she looked or dressed. Kneeling on the spongy pink-and-green carpeted floor of the mosque's dingy basement—the area designated for women while the men prayed in the airier and more welcoming space above—was where I would ask Allah for guidance, just as my mother did. There was a kinship among the women who occupied that space together, as many of them resented being treated as second-class citizens within their own faith. Our only access to any ideological dialogue about the verses of the Quran came by way of a TV screen projecting what male elders deemed worthy of our discussion. Women were not asked to share their thoughts on how the teachings of the Quran played out in their lives. So for that kinship to be broken, for those generous embraces that once cushioned us to be taken away, was especially devastating.

One of the reasons I had sent El-Farouk an email introducing myself and asking to be part of the Friday congregation was that I missed being in the presence of other Muslims. I used to look forward to attending mosque with my parents and sisters. Getting ready together was one of the few family rituals we brought over with us from Pakistan. My mom would spend hours getting my sisters and me dolled up, as though for a red-carpet entrance. She would oil our hair the night before with Dabur Amla hair oil—a staple in many South Asian households—and secure our thick curls in a tight braid so that after we washed it the next morning our hair would gleam for days. Similar, care went into our outfits, each shalwar kameez brightly coloured and carefully ironed. Only the trendiest ones, which relatives and family friends had brought back from Pakistan, were worn to mosque.

Some of my most treasured childhood memories are of Islamic traditions that brought me closer to my family, such as breaking a light fast with cousins in Lahore—fasting for just part of the day to feel a sense of camaraderie with the grown-ups, who fast until after sunset during Ramadan.

Even now, nothing makes me feel more centred than listening to a beautiful recitation of the call to prayer, whether I'm in my Toronto apartment or the crowded streets of Cihangir.

But for most of my twenties, Islam felt like a parent dishing out conditional love: I had no right to call myself Muslim because I'm queer and don't wear the hijab. After more than a decade of deprivation, I was spiritually hungry. Although I maintained a private relationship with Allah, I longed for a non-judgmental spiritual community where I could meet others like myself.

I had also reached out to El-Farouk because, despite identifying as queer for years, I still felt like an outsider within the LGBTQ community. I had naively assumed that no longer keeping my queer identity a secret would help me find my people. In reality, it pushed me further into the hole of isolation. It seemed that no one in the queer spaces I visited—dance parties, art shows, Pride events—was curious about why there were hardly any people of colour—and hardly any Muslims—in their midst. I felt even more invisible.

The prayer was to be held in an unassuming building in the heart of Toronto's gay village. There was a blizzard that night. Taking the elevator up, I had no idea what to expect. I took a wrong turn that led me to a women's health centre, and after I found my way back to the entrance the receptionist noticed me lingering, uncertain. "Jumah?" she mouthed. She gave me a generous smile and pointed to a pile of winter boots and puffy parkas gathered outside a room to my left. I had arrived at my new mosque.

I recognized El-Farouk from news stories. As the crowd swelled, he stared at his laptop on the floor, greeting people on Skype who had joined from around the world. Attendees warmed themselves with paper cups full of piping hot passion fruit tea from the large jugs placed in the centre of the room.

Too shy yet to join them, I silently observed. My eyes were still adjusting to the startling sight of acceptance, as though I'd just had a blindfold ripped off. I worried that not wearing a hijab would result in a stern lecture from El-Farouk, but his attention had turned to his handsome husband, Troy, who had just come in from the blizzard outside wrapped in an oversized knitted cardigan. I dipped my toes in slowly by letting my embroidered head scarf fall gently over my shoulders, revealing my ombré curls. I wondered if I would get looks from the others. I didn't.

As I sat cross-legged on the prayer mat and stared out the window, I could hardly believe I was coming back to my faith in the same neighbourhood where I attended my first drag show. Minutes away from a cluster of lesbian bars and leather clubs, I was meeting myself again in my thirties.

Sitting next to me was Rashida, a middle-aged butch from Egypt dressed in a plaid shirt and a ski jacket. Short blond curls poked out from under the black beanie she wore to cover her head for the prayer or, probably more likely, to protect against the bitter cold. Back home, she had been a renowned Arabic singer, regularly casting spells on her loyal fans with a melancholic voice that soothed the broken-hearted. She now needed consoling herself, after word got out that she was gay and had a lover. It became evident to her, through regular threats, that she had no choice but to flee the country and to leave behind her lover, her family, and the life she had built. There was also Sam, a gender-nonconforming Iranian immigrant. Sitting across from me were Mahmood and Omar, two young transgender refugees from Algeria. Mahmood's parents thought he'd left to study abroad and had no idea he'd transitioned; he was afraid to tell them.

One of the most striking differences from the traditional mosques I attended when I was younger was that people of all genders prayed side by side. Muslims of all orientations and racial backgrounds shared the same space, the same floor.

Before the sermon began we were all handed a sheet of house rules, which highlighted that we were not to argue with others about the validity of their faith, since all Muslims experience Islam in different ways. After all, Islam is not a monolithic religion. Although all of us in that room viewed and experienced Islam through a queer lens, the version of Islam we each practised was very much shaped by what also set us apart: geography, culture, race, class, and history.

As I was still soaking in every detail that challenged my idea of what a mosque could look like, a black trans woman in her twenties got up from the floor to give a beautiful recitation of the *adhan*, the call to prayer. I discreetly surveyed the room to see whether anyone else shared my emotional reaction to this powerful reclamation and profound queering of the traditional call to prayer, but most looked meditative and focused. I tried to hold back my tears—for the first time I was witnessing a version of Islam I could be a part of. After being scolded and frozen out, I now felt that Islam was welcoming me back into its arms. It had been an awful lonely time, and I was glad to be in the company of people who didn't ask me to change who I was in order to share space with them. I had finally found my people.

As we all started praying together, kneeling before God, I was surprised to find the prayers I had abandoned trickling off my tongue as though they'd never left. They'd been inside me all along, nudging me toward this moment. I was emboldened to think about what kind of relationship

I wanted with Islam—something that had never been an option growing up. You were born a Muslim and had to abide by certain rules and standards if you were to retain your membership. For so long, I had lived under the glare of disapproval. The heady realization that I could still have a place in a faith that had previously rejected me felt shocking. I was witnessing that which I had only ever imagined: a queer utopia of sorts. A fantasy of being accepted and being seen.

My subsequent visits to Unity Mosque felt like group therapy sessions punctuated by familiar religious rituals. Each time, my personal relationship with Islam was restored a little bit more, and my experience of always having felt like an outcast within Islam was validated. I'd never felt more Muslim than I did among my fellow outsiders, who came from all over the world and who each practised Islam in their own individual ways. There were people covered in tattoos and piercings, while others were wrapped in traditional burkas or chose to wear the hijab. Some prayed five times a day, while others, like me, prayed only occasionally. Yet we had come together because we were unhappy with how queer Muslims are made to feel in mainstream mosques—as though we were all sinners who were going to hell. Many of us had been made to feel rejected by Allah at times when we needed him most. I loved that we were questioning and reimagining not just what it means to be Muslim in the twenty-first century but how to apply Islamic teachings to our present-day lives. I looked to these peers to see how they dealt with rejection from their families and with Islamophobia from non-Muslims.

Unlike my past encounters with the faith, like my childhood experience of being marginalized for being Ahmadi, this new reclamation didn't feel hierarchical. No one was dictating the right or wrong way to be Muslim. I started to wonder if it had been unfair of me to write off my religion because of how some of its followers, including my own parents, had made me feel. I now saw that I could carve out a place for myself that provided me with the spiritual nourishment I needed to weather life's hurdles.

Occasionally, if I was getting to know someone romantically, I would invite them to join me at the mosque. Understanding why that place means so much to me was the key to understanding who I am at my core. It was also a way for me to gauge how accepting a potential partner would be of the role spirituality plays in my life.

For me, practising Islam feeds my desire to understand the beauty and complexity of the universe and to treat everyone, regardless of their beliefs, with respect. My faith inspires kindness, patience, and self-reflection in my daily interactions. Relearning how to pray—focusing on the words and the prayer steps, such as kneeling in front of God in *sajda*—taught me that completely surrendering yourself to something you love is a gift. In fact, it's in the getting lost that you find yourself.

Energized by my experience at Unity Mosque, I found myself thinking of ways I could prolong this giddy inspiration and turn it into something meaningful. I knew I wanted to capture the spirit of the space and the people I encountered in it. My desire to work on a project that was true to me served as my only compass.

So it was no surprise that I gravitated toward photography. Poring over images in magazines had been my salvation as a teenager and even in the past year had helped rescue me from some dark times. After months of emotional abuse, I'd left a girlfriend who regularly gaslighted me and made me doubt my own intuition. I felt betrayed that a woman could exhibit such misogynistic behaviour. Over the course of our relationship, I'd forgotten what happiness looked like. My face had become gaunt, my eyes glazed over. Looking at old pictures stuck to my refrigerator—laughing with friends at summer cottages, hotel photobooth strips from late nights dancing to disco anthems—I was struck by how distant that version of myself seemed. I started making a digital collage of photos of queer people laughing and looking genuinely elated, many of them shot by queer fashion photographer Cass Bird. The images implanted a new hope in me that being queer can also be a cause for joy. That you can create a community for yourself when society denies you one. The contents of that folder on my laptop marked HAPPY eventually gave me the key to starting a portrait series.

The idea for the project had another seed: I wasn't seeing the queer Muslim narratives I was hungry for occupying the spaces I frequented. It seemed that because we didn't fit the popular imagination's perceptions of Muslims, we simply didn't exist. I wanted to convey the countless narratives found within Islam and explore unfamiliar territory to create a broader, more multi-layered understanding of Muslims. And I would incorporate the aesthetic of glossy magazines and teen feminist zines that had inspired my own personal style growing up. Once the idea had crystallized, its magnetic pull was irresistible.

Since I'd been working as a fashion editor and writer for years, I had a solid foundation to start from. I'd thrown myself into working on features that emphasized beauty and lightness—an antidote to the weight of trauma I'd carried since childhood. Being surrounded by photographers, stylists, and hair and makeup artists helped me develop an eye. I was often tasked with coming up with story ideas and collaborating with models and crew to execute our vision. As most fashion editors do, I would bring a stack of tear sheets—often the work of *Vogue* greats like Steven Meisel, Edward Enninful, Pat McGrath, and Peter Lindbergh—to help guide the shoots. When I expressed an interest in photography, friends I'd met on set offered to give me lessons, thrilled to teach me about everything from lighting to lenses.

To better learn about the technical side of things, I took photography classes after work. I would bring pages torn from some of my favourite magazines and ask my teacher how to recreate the looks. I quickly discovered that a lot of the photography that resonated with me was shot on a 50 mm lens, which is what I continue to shoot my subjects with. I love the intimate feel it lends to portraits. Everything in the background is blurred, and the rich textures of the subject become the main focus. I started spending most evenings at the nearby university library, reading up on Dorothea Lange, Henri Cartier-Bresson, Gordon Parks, and Diane Arbus. I loved how these photographers zoomed in on subjects that highlighted the realities of their times—whether they were African Americans during the civil rights movement or the homeless and unemployed of the Great Depression.

One of the things I loved most about photography is how accessible it is as a language. Because English was not my first language, I often struggled to articulate subtle feelings I was used to talking about in Urdu, which is a much more poetic language. As a kid, I found comfort in cheesy pop songs by the Spice Girls and the Backstreet Boys because I could grasp the simplicity of their lyrics. My inability to access the language in a deep and layered way prevented me from fully expressing the flood of emotions and frustrations I'd felt as an immigrant in a new country. Our understanding of the interior lives of those who are not like us is contingent on their ability to articulate themselves in the language we know. The further removed people are from proficiency in that language, the less likely they are to be understood as complex individuals. The audience often fills in the blanks with their own preconceptions. But visual language is more easily parsed and a much more democratic form of communication. We're bombarded with images through advertising, television, and social media—consuming images is part of our daily life.

Much has been written in academia about queer Muslims, but often the ideas and findings are disseminated by scholars who have far more privilege than the subjects of their work. I've sat on panels where I felt excluded from conversations by the barrier of academic jargon. It seemed as though meaningful dialogue was available only to those with a PhD. In this way, the language is inaccessible to those who need to be comforted most. Queer Muslims who fear for their lives every day—while walking down the streets of Punjabi villages or meeting a potential love interest for the first time in Tehran through a dating app—might not have the tools to understand the language written by academics in Ivy League schools.

Representation is a critical way for people to recognize that their experiences—even if invisible in the mainstream—are valid. For the longest time queer Muslims have been made to feel that our fears, pains, needs, and desires are not valid because, before the existence of social media, we largely lived in isolation from others who shared them. But the popularity of Instagram, Tumblr, and hashtags has enabled us to find our communities and create our tribes, connecting with and empowering one another.

Representation presented another challenge: historically, photography has been prohibited within Islam. Prophet Muhammad has been noted as saying, "The most severely punished people on the Day of Resurrection will be those who make images." Not surprisingly, given that very explicit message, it's almost impossible to find photographic evidence of the existence of queer Muslims. As I researched historical images of queer movements and icons in libraries and on social media, I wasn't able to find a single person who identified as Muslim. But lack of representation of course doesn't mean that they haven't existed alongside other queer activists in the twentieth century.

In the beginning, it wasn't easy getting people to agree to be part of my project. I could understand why: as Muslims, we're used to being exploited at the hands of others. I myself am wary when asked to represent a group of people. That's a lot of responsibility to take on, and in the past, the portrayal of Muslims has by and large been negative. For example, Media Tenor, a research institute that evaluates data for NGOs and governments, reviewed media coverage by NBC, CBS, and Fox from 2007 to 2013 and found that over 80 percent of it on NBC and CBS was negative, while Fox's coverage of Muslims largely focused on news about international terrorism and conflict.

At times, it felt as though all my hard work and good intentions were simply not enough to move my project forward. I encountered a lot of hesitation from older queer Muslims, who felt they'd had to make a choice earlier in life—they could be either Muslim or openly queer, but not both—and ultimately left Islam because they didn't see room for themselves. It took a lot of effort to convince them that my intention was to create a platform where queer Muslims could be their authentic selves. It was also difficult to persuade people to be part of the project simply because there was no precedent for it. And I encountered resistance from non-Muslim queers, too. Sometimes we Canadians live in a bubble, seduced by the illusion of equality. Many didn't see the need for a project highlighting the struggles of queer Muslims because they were under the impression that things were great for all LGBTQ people in the country. After all, we were one of the first countries to legalize same-sex marriage. And if being a queer Muslim weren't my lived experience, perhaps I would have believed that too. But I knew the struggle all too well. I felt it every time I was in queer spaces and searched for faces that looked like my own.

One day, when I was particularly frustrated because I felt I wasn't making any progress, I received an email from Zainab, a transgender woman from Tunisia who was going to university in Montreal. She wrote that she had grown up in a Muslim family, and that although she still identified as a Muslim, her relationship with Islam had changed over the years. "My gender identity made things somewhat complex and it's hard to find an equilibrium between some conservative religious beliefs and a liberal and queer view on things. I'm glad to be part of your project. I always supported queer visibility, especially in Muslim and Arab communities," she said. I had found my first subject.

I immediately booked a train ticket to Montreal. This ended up becoming a typical experience for me. People would contact me, and I would use the grant money I got to launch the project to travel to their city soon after. I rented an apartment in the Mile End neighbourhood, and Zainab and I arranged to meet at a train station close by. After waiting twenty minutes on a park bench outside the station, flipping through a newspaper, I noticed someone walking toward me. It was as if Zainab had stepped out of a Christian Schad painting. She was wearing a long black peacoat over a black skirt and had an asymmetrical wavy bob. Her lipstick matched the jet black curls that peeked out from under a black wide-brimmed hat. She strutted toward me in her sky-high platform heels, a brooch on her lapel that read GOTH PARK. Even her nails were black. It was love at first sight. I was flattered she'd dressed up so flawlessly for our portrait session. When we hugged, I caught a whiff of many familiar smells that reminded me of walking through the perfumy markets in Pakistan as a child: jasmine oil, neroli, and sandalwood. When Zainab discovered that I had never been to Montreal she was excited to show me around, and we spent most of the day walking about the city together. That became an integral part of the process with all my subjects. It was important for me to get to know them in their environment before I photographed them. I wanted to know what they'd been through, what they'd seen, and what they were seeking so that I could capture them in a way that reflected their spirit.

Since Zainab was very particular about how she wanted to be portrayed, we waited until the wind calmed down and her hair fell over her eye just so. She wanted to be photographed in front of Montreal's grand old churches, and I happily obliged. It turned out that years of coordinating big photo shoots and putting models at ease had trained me well for making queer Muslim refugees who had escaped wars and violence feel comfortable in front of the camera. Some subjects, like Zainab, were naturally comfortable and confidently displayed themselves before the lens, but at many shoots I would have to come up with creative ways to protect the subjects' identities, as many feared for their safety if their queerness became known. I believed that however the subjects wished to be documented was part of the larger story I was trying to tell.

In the short amount of time we were together, I felt I had come to know Zainab intimately: her work, her life, and what she had gone through back home in Tunisia. This happened almost all the time with my subjects. Given the reason we were meeting, they all felt comfortable telling me personal details about their lives, and it was always sad to say goodbye. I often felt as though I were leaving family behind—and in a way, I was.

When I asked Zainab what advice she would give to young queer Muslims who are looking for support and community, her response gave me chills. I still turn to her words for motivation:

"We have always been here, it's just that the world wasn't ready for us yet. Today, with all the political upheavals in the Muslim World, some of us, those who are not daily threatened with death or rejection, have to speak for others. They have to tell stories of a community that is either denied or scorned. Together, through facing distinct realities, we should be united—united in the desire to be, in the desire to enjoy being free, safe, and happy. It is not going to be easy and one may never reach a reconciliation with oneself (or with religion), but at least we should care for each other. In face of the challenges, our sense of community and our shared aspirations for a better world should make us stronger."

eleven

There's a house in the middle of downtown Toronto, a five-minute walk from the main art gallery, a few blocks south of a big university campus. It's an Edwardian building, painted heritage red like the spines of nineteenth-century books, with white trim around the windows and doors. There's a generous patio, large enough to accommodate impromptu al fresco lunches in late summer, when no one's in any particular rush. The house manages to offer both the space to reflect on a new moon and a grounding perspective to weather life's next string of challenges, to consider the smallness of the self and the largeness of the universe. *Whatever has happened to you has happened before*, the house consoles. The street is extremely quiet. It's hard to believe it's only a few minutes away from the bustling commercial centre of the city.

It's one of many row houses on the street built in the early 1900s. They were largely inhabited by European Jews until the 1960s, when Chinese families moved into the neighbourhood after the city's original Chinatown, farther east, was demolished. The house isn't very tall; the top floor is low enough that in the summer, when the bay windows are flung open to let the breeze in, you can see into the bedroom to admire the antique gold wallpaper. An imposing white oak protects the house year-round, as it has for a century's worth of immigrant families. *Stay away*, it says to possible intruders. But when the branches are bare, you can make out a person reading at the windowsill or an older couple sitting out front, watching the new world go by. Sometimes there are two empty glasses on the porch; other times, a pair of well-worn slippers.

I see my mother. She's in the backyard, staring into the garden: her oasis amid all the concrete. She makes good use of what little space she has. It's here that life makes sense when, farther afield, not much else does: unnecessary wars, Islamophobia. The calming greens are punctuated by pops of vibrant colour that remind her of home—veronicas that flower in early summer, butterflies swarming the pincushions. Off the alleyway are dozens of coach houses owned by bankers, ad execs, and professors who are subjected to a litany of strong odours wafting from our property: lilacs, cumin, roses, and once a year, a goat roasting on the pit for Eid. But my mother doesn't make any apologies. "This is Canada," she says. "Let these people get used to us desis." She snaps a handful of mint leaves for chutney later. The smell of nihari simmering on the stove fills the kitchen and the narrow hallway that leads to the backyard.

Every Thursday after prayer, she throws a small dinner party. She invites old friends, mostly neighbours who've been living here for decades, as well as new immigrants who've made a habit of dropping by her makeshift mosque in the basement—refugees from Pakistan, Turkey, Somalia, and Egypt. For many of them, it's their first time under the same roof as non-Muslims. This gathering is important to my mother. It's her chance to give back to people who desperately crave what she lacked: a chance for connection away from the only home they ever knew. As she looks across the room, she's proud of the community she's built over the years and her contribution toward enriching it. Our home is one of the only places many of the refugees feel safe.

My father is away on a business trip. He's an engineer, and he isn't devalued or demeaned by colleagues who are younger than him. My parents bought the house to be close to the universities their daughters planned on attending. One sister is getting her degree in women's studies while the other is studying political science (she plans to go to law school after getting her bachelor's degree). My brother, the youngest, is nowhere to be found—probably on his skate-board somewhere in Kensington Market. He knows he has to be home by Maghrib prayer, though. Journalism school is a bit challenging, and the midterms are driving me nuts. But it could be worse, I suppose. My parents are able to pay my tuition, and it was generous of them to let me stay in the house for the next two years as I apply for internships in Latin America and South Asia. I'm keen to go back to Pakistan to report on the queer community there.

When my brother finally shows up, just in time for dinner, he drops the news that he's considering taking a year off after high school to travel. "I just want to experience the world first and be sure about what I want, you know?" he says between mouthfuls of cucumber salad. "I'd like to make an informed decision."

"Whatever you do, we will support you," my dad says.

And my parents do support him. In fact, sometimes they're a little *too* accommodating. The year before, he transformed the basement into a performance venue, putting on rock shows for his friends until the neighbours started complaining. To my surprise, I don't actually dislike his music. I can tell he's heavily influenced by Bauhaus, who I used to play all the time when I was younger, although he'd never admit it.

"You can do it, Bilal," we all say in an encouraging voice, as though we've rehearsed. We think it's important for him to have the time and space to figure out what he truly wants to do with his life. After all, the three of us sisters were the beneficiaries of similar support from our parents. "You can do it!" their voices echoed as each of us decided to take chances and visit unfamiliar horizons, bolstered by their confidence in our ability to figure it out as we went along.

Our house is filled with books. Nabokov, Baldwin, Didion, Woolf, Plath, Kincaid, Sontag. "Books are where you will find yourself," my mother would say whenever she sensed we'd lost our footing. Like when I had my heart broken by Evelyn, the first girlfriend I ever introduced to my parents. My mother pulled various tomes off the shelves—books about disasters of all kinds, heartbreaks so catastrophic they put mine in perspective. "Jaan, it helps to find solace in the larger universe, especially when your internal world isn't hospitable," she said, hoping that the advice would stick. "Sometimes that is how you come back to yourself."

Beyond the library, you can see the dining room, where my father plays chess with one of his old chess partners while they catch up on life, real estate, and the ludicrous price of oil.

This house gave us the space to figure out who we were supposed to be. To look inward, to listen to our intuition.

But this house does not exist.

I've always been obsessed with the idea of home. I'll catch myself imagining the childhood homes of people I admire:

Did Hilton Als's family eat meals together around the dinner table? What elements in Rebecca Solnit's house might hint at her mother's narcissistic tendencies? What might others conclude about *me* based on the fact that my mom used her bathtub as storage for unopened beauty products? A person's childhood home is the prologue to their story. It contains clues to the inner workings of their minds, their specific view of the world.

It's no wonder I was so fascinated. The kind of home I imagine—one that offers stability and encouragement and the space to learn and grow as an individual—is a luxury I never had growing up. Before coming to Canada, I devoted weeks to imagining what our new house would look like. Drawing elaborate floor plans, as I'd watched my father do for the houses he built in Pakistan, was my way of literally visualizing a future. My scribbles were my security, a reminder that at the other end of all this uncertainty was comfort. It would all be worth it. But once we arrived, I saw my parents stripped of their power and authority—how could they possibly nurture my interests and talents when their primary concern was our survival? So I had to look elsewhere to find my mentors. Feeling forever out of place, I spent my formative years in a state of suspended development, always searching. Eventually I would find writers who were able to put my fears and insecurities into words, and artists who would inspire me to do the same, but for many years I was an outsider looking in, compelled by a mix of wonder and envy.

To me, friends and acquaintances who'd grown up with parents who were active in their communities, who took them on summer vacations and hosted backyard barbecues, were as rare and foreign as movie stars and Olympic athletes—I listened to their tales with awe. What was it like to grow up not having to worry about whether your parents could pay the next month's rent, or put food on the table? How would the absence of fear have guided my life choices? Would I have taken more risks instead of seeking out the safety I so deeply craved? Am I better off for having struggled to figure out where I belonged?

I don't know what it's like to live in a place where I have roots. Where old women see you on the street and remark that you have your grandmother's eyes. Where the Pakistani grocer around the corner asks how your father's doing when you stop by to pick up a box of gulab jamun. I never had quick family visits with grandparents, aunts, uncles, and cousins to heal wounds and provide relief from the constant exercise of having to introduce myself. No ancestors who've left footprints for me to follow or passed down stories to serve as a roadmap. I'm new here.

Where I live, the Sikh shop owner does not know my father or my grandfather. But, when months go by without any connection to my early years in Pakistan, seeing him at the counter when I go in to buy cigarettes or Indian sweets offers some comfort. We roll our eyes at the skateboarders who, clearly high, point to a tray of samosas and ask, "What's that?" And so I've developed a habit of sourcing out familiarity in unfamiliar places. When I'm visiting a new neighbourhood, I seek out the brown people. Just their existence is enough to put me at ease. Sometimes I find them without even looking. On my first trip to Paris, I went for a nighttime stroll and was overcome with a disorienting sense of déjà vu. The next day, once my jetlag had worn off, I realized I was staying in what was essentially Little Pakistan. The restaurants in the area all specialized in Punjabi cooking from my hometown. No wonder I was disoriented; I had one foot in a foreign city and the other in my mother's kitchen in Lahore.

"Where are you from?" is a question that can make many brown people uncomfortable, particularly second- and third-generation Canadians, who are perhaps less likely to have felt othered than first-generation immigrants and refugees who left the countries they were born in. But I can empathize with the longing to connect while being in a constant state of disconnection, so I don't mind being asked. And yet I can't help wondering: will my niece Zoe, born in Canada and surrounded by family—aunts, uncles, cousins, grandparents, and parents who are equipped to give her the tools she needs to prepare for life—search for the same kind of familiarity as she makes her way through new streets?

In my thirties, still weighed down by these feelings of displacement, by the trauma of growing up without safety, without home, I started inching toward therapy. Terrified by what I might find when I confronted my past, I'd put it off for years. I was certain I would unravel. So I kept myself busy with work and my photo project and my friends—so busy that I wouldn't notice the parts of me I'd left untended. I had to survive; I had to keep going.

With the encouragement of my sisters, who insisted I seek a good therapist to help as I revisited and unpacked my childhood, I decided it was finally time. As usual, they were right: after every appointment—during which my therapist covers me in a blanket, and I detail critical events that continue to haunt me—I leave lighter. When I find myself getting angry about something that happened twenty-five or thirty years ago, when I had no control over my life or even my body, I think about her reminders to simply breathe.

Re-parent yourself is another of her favourite mantras for me. She asks the child Samra to come out and say whatever she needs to say to me. She even had me write a letter to her as an exercise. At first I thought it was an impossible task, but after a few sessions and my therapist's insistent coaxing, the terrified seven-year-old me—shaggy short hair, blue shalwar kameez—started following me around like a shadow. Now she won't leave me alone. She wants to make herself heard, she wants to be comforted, and she wants to know that I will protect her. She wants me to tell her that she doesn't have to do anything she doesn't want to. And she wants to tell me to not be upset with my mother. To forgive her. Whenever a feeling of anxiety or fear creeps into my thoughts, I gently console the seven-year-old instead of the adult. "Don't worry—it'll be all right," I say. "I'll take care of you." And I mean it.

Mothers know. It's frustrating—eerie, even—how easily my mother can sense that a storm is brewing inside of me. Sometimes she even sees it before I do. It's like having a psychological intruder.

For weeks after I came out in a very public way—by writing about being queer in a piece for *The Guardian*—I kept checking my phone, expecting a call from my parents any minute. Every buzz and beep set me on edge. Although my siblings had known for years, my parents still had no idea that I was queer. I wondered if a relative would send them a link to the piece, sparking a confrontation.

The phone call never came.

Rehabilitating my relationship with my mother had become my priority. I wanted to stop hiding parts of myself from her—and by extension stop me from hiding parts of myself from others. Working on the photo project had empowered me in ways I'd never expected. Although not everyone has the privilege or the need to declare their queerness, for me it felt incredibly liberating, especially because not many Muslims come out—many suffer horrible backlash and danger for doing so. For once, there was a term that summed me up like nothing else had before. I thought: What if I could lessen someone else's pain of feeling like they didn't belong simply by presenting my authentic queer self instead of hiding? Perhaps merely daring to exist openly was a radical act.

Funnily enough, it was around this time that my parents moved to—of all places—Toronto's gay village. ("Sorry I'm late for Eid, I was stuck in the gay pride parade" is one thing I never thought I'd hear my mother say.) Their highrise condo is nestled between fetish stores and clubs where people have sex in dimly lit bathrooms while techno music throbs in the background. It was one of the few places they could find that fit their specific criteria.

Walking arm in arm down Church Street with my mother, who has transitioned from wearing the burka to the hijab, brings me tremendous joy. She doesn't show any sign of being fazed as we pass rainbow flags and same-sex couples holding hands. It delights me to see how we've both changed over the years. Or could it be that I was only just starting to see her?

One afternoon not long after my *Guardian* piece was published, my mother asked me if I wanted to join her and my brother for lunch. We met at an Indian restaurant down-town—it was deserted after the lunch-hour rush, save for the three of us. When our appetizers arrived, my mother put her hand on mine, adjusted her hijab, and looked me in the eyes.

"Samra, I feel like there is something you are not telling me," she said.

My brother, sitting across from us, mouthed *no* in that specific way of siblings who are bound by the secrets they keep from their parents. Perhaps he thought the news would be too much for her to absorb. Although my siblings supported me, they believed that my mother—an obser-vant Muslim who still wears a hijab in public—wouldn't accept my queerness. They felt they needed to protect her. Admittedly, so did I.

In that moment, I wondered what made me any differ-ent from those who projected their own judgments onto Muslim women who wore the hijab or the burka. I had no evidence that she would disapprove. Never in my life had I caught her saying anything remotely homophobic or trans-phobic. And she wouldn't have, because to her, being hate-ful in any way goes against her religious beliefs. This was a woman who would recite the motto of the Ahmadiyya community—*Love for all, hatred for none*—whenever someone directed an Islamophobic remark at us on the street or in shopping malls or grocery stores.

A few seconds went by as I wrestled with the prospect of finally being honest with her and giving her a chance to accept me. I also understood that if she chose *not* to accept me, I didn't have that much to lose; by this point in my life, I didn't rely on my parents for anything.

Finally I just blurted it out. "Mom, I'm queer." I searched her face for a reaction—or signs of an impending heart attack. We looked at each other in silence while my brother looked on anxiously.

"Okay," she said. "I still love you."

It's what she said next that I wasn't prepared for.

"So . . . how do you have sex?"

For the next few weeks, my mother sent me regular text messages telling me how much she loved me and how much she appreciated my opening up to her. My worst-case scenario never materialized: she hadn't told me I was going to hell or tried to convince me that my queerness was just a phase, and she wasn't going to cut me out of family gatherings. For the first time in my life, I felt the warmth of unconditional love.

Soon I was telling my mom about everyone I dated: femmes, butches, trans-masculine-identified people. Each time she'd ask the same questions she might have asked if I were dating a nice Muslim boy: Do they come from a good family? Are they respectful? Do they make you happy?

I'm hoping that over time, as we fully re-enter each other's lives, we'll fill in the gaps left by those missing years. Although I'm intimately aware of the journey I took to get where I am, I'm not sure what kind of self-realizations and epiphanies have contributed to my mother's growth. What happened in between arranging her teenage daughter's marriage to her cousin and accepting that she now dates all kinds of queer people? To better understand myself, I need to understand how she got here. I intend to spend the rest of the time she's alive finding out.

When I was a heartbroken mess after splitting up with Evelyn, a butch I'd introduced to my mother as a "friend," she held me the way I needed to be held, and I realized how long I'd been craving that embrace.

"I didn't think she was right for you," she said as I sobbed into her chest. "You deserve someone much better."

She continues to prove to me that she accepts me and loves me unconditionally, in big ways and little ways, too. When I told her about my photo project, she smiled knowingly.

"I get it," she said. "You're trying to make Muslims who are treated unfairly feel like they are part of Islam. That's very Muslim of you."

twelve

On an otherwise unremarkable day in the fall of 2016, I stood in a crowded auditorium at the University of North Carolina, poised to deliver a keynote address about queer Muslims in America. My talk, entitled "Spirituality as a Radical Tool," had been scheduled months before, but the election results had cast a shadow over the event. It was November 9, and Donald Trump was the new president of the United States.

I'd never been to North Carolina, so I did some research before my trip and discovered it had been home to many people I admired: Nina Simone, John Coltrane, Thelonious Monk, George Clinton, André Leon Talley. Eager to make the most of my time there, I'd put out a call on social media for people who might be interested in participating in my photo project, which is how I found Saba and Laila, a married queer Muslim couple who lived in Durham among a thriving community of artists and activists. We arranged to meet the day after my keynote.

The university put me up in a hotel close to campus, and the night before, I rehearsed my speech with the TV tuned to the election coverage. I went over my lines about how important it was to share the stories of a diverse range of queer Muslims around the world in order to show that Islam is not a monolithic religion, and about the importance of providing Muslims, especially queer ones, a platform to share their stories in their own words. I made notes on how crucial it is to add faces to the very human experiences we Muslims go through in a world that insists on dehumanizing Islam. *"I wanted my subjects to look straight into the eyes of the audience and tell the stories of their struggles, fears, triumphs, love, and courage in their own words."*

I went into the bathroom and rehearsed in front of the mirror while the talking heads continued to speculate in the background. I visualized myself taking the stage (the organizers had asked which song I wanted played before I was introduced, and I requested Gil Scott-Heron's "I'm New Here") and tried to imagine what sorts of faces I'd see in the audience. Restless and anxious, I abandoned my run-through midway and began pacing the room, peeking into closets and cupboards. There, in the top drawer of the nightstand, was a compact, gold-embossed Bible. It seemed to me a little presumptuous that every hotel visitor would need a copy—that it was as essential as a clothes hanger or an ironing board. I snapped a photo and texted it

WE HAVE ALWAYS BEEN HERE

to my sister. "That's what they do in America," she replied, unfazed. Suddenly a news anchor was announcing that Trump, who had built so much of his platform on inciting hate for Muslims and immigrants, was predicted to win the election. I watched in shock as the results continued to roll in. A reality-TV star would be deciding the fate of the most powerful country in the world. In disbelief, I set my alarm for an hour later and took a nap. When I awoke, Trump's victory had gone from hypothetical to almost certain: the nightmare was real.

I'd been working on my photo project for a couple of years, and by 2016 it was garnering a considerable amount of media coverage. The tipping point was sudden and surprising, and the response was beyond my wildest dreams. One day I was just a girl with a camera and an idea, and the next my work was being exhibited at the Victoria and Albert Museum in London. The exposure began to guide the direction of my journalism: instead of writing about the best moisturizers for the décolletage and finding a scent based on your star sign, I was now writing about race, Islamophobia, the concept of community, spirituality, and access to AIDS research from a queer Muslim lens for outlets like *The Guardian*, Public Radio International, and *The Advocate*.

Soon enough I was getting booked for speaking engagements, like the one in North Carolina. I'd pack my bags and show up in different cities around the globe, ready to talk about the subjects I photographed and what their experiences revealed about Islam and the treatment of Muslims. My work was especially of interest in Europe and America, where Islamophobia had escalated in recent years. I was invited to participate in exhibitions and panels in Oslo, Brussels, Berlin, and certain parts of the U.S. (Even though I wasn't a citizen, I was often asked to comment on the challenges queer Muslims face in America.) These opportunities allowed me to form friendships with queer Muslims all over, an experience that expanded my idea of community, which was no longer limited by geography. It was also a great vantage point from which to observe how varied people's relationships with Islam could be.

I arrived in Istanbul shortly after Turkey banned Pride events under Erdoğan's rule. Queer Muslims I met there were understandably disillusioned with Islam, since their rights were compromised by authorities daily. Although they were born to Muslim parents, they didn't understand why as a queer-identified person I would choose to call myself Muslim. The interest in racial justice and equality that had guided my work was visibly absent from their activism. Many of the queer Muslims I'd met in America and Europe dealt with racism on top of the homophobia, transphobia, and Islamophobia they continually experience. It was important to me to ensure that the voices of queer Muslims who were black and trans were included in my project, to show the additional layers of systemic discrimination beyond Islamophobia. Unlike the queer Muslims I met in Turkey, many in Paris, Berlin, and the U.S. proudly wore religious markers like the hijab, or an Allah necklace, as an act of resistance to various burgeoning forms of Islamophobia. For some, it's a gauge to determine whether someone is worth their time and respect.

I was constantly reminded that, just as there are many sects of Islam practised throughout the world, different geographic and cultural factors dictate the injustices queer Muslims face and thus shape their activism. I remember a conversation I had with a young Iranian refugee I met in Istanbul who'd escaped to the city after being targeted by the morality police in Iran. Eventually, he made his way to the U.S. For years he lived in a constant state of fear that he would be killed for being gay. Yet when we discussed the discrimination African Americans face in his adopted home, he was reluctant to see how a country that had welcomed him could be cruel to others because of their race. As our conversation went on, I discovered that he had never witnessed the racial-based injustices blacks face in Iran and Istanbul. He hadn't met many queers who were of a different race. For him, the realities that made him fear for his life and feel disenfranchised were not connected to his race—only to his sexuality.

After each trip, I'd return home with a renewed sense of purpose. In between my travels, social media played an important role when face-to-face support wasn't available. Many in the queer community were still reeling from the Pulse nightclub shooting in Orlando, and the far-reaching networks we'd created offered some solace amid all the sadness and confusion. Convinced of the power of affirming one's queerness in dark times, I took another big step forward: I told my dad that I was queer. I was accompanying him to a doctor's appointment—he'd been dealing with a health issue that had him in and out of the hospital for various tests and checkups—and we got to talking about my twenties, when our estrangement was at its peak. I told him how depressed I'd been, and how my marriage fell apart because it was preventing me from being my authentic queer self. I don't know if I expected him to understand, but his response, economical as it was, is something I won't forget. "You can't help it," he said. "It's just who you are."

The morning of my talk, as I headed down to the hotel lobby for breakfast, I shared the elevator with two visibly shaken twentysomethings.

"Can you believe it?" one said.

"This is a nightmare, right? Trump isn't actually going to be our president," the other replied.

"I can't believe it either," I chimed in. "It's surreal." I desperately needed to share my shock with other human beings.

"We're so sorry," one of them offered, and the other added, "This isn't our fault. We didn't vote for him!"

Midterms were in full swing, and dozens of students were cuddling puppies in the courtyard when I arrived on campus. The university representative who'd picked me up explained that the puppies were meant to comfort stressed-out students during exams. I wondered how many of them were looking to soothe a whole new kind of anxiety that morning.

The atmosphere in the auditorium was sombre. I scanned the audience and saw that many of the attendees were young people of colour, and many of them wore the hijab. The faculty made some opening remarks acknowledging how traumatizing the election results might be for many of the students and noting the various support services available to them. I thought of how different—how celebratory—the mood would have been if another candidate had won. But then I realized that this was exactly why I'd launched my project in the first place: to speak to mostly young people who were made to feel that they didn't belong and who experienced, each day, the brutal realities of Islamophobia, racism, homophobia, and transphobia. In North Carolina at the time, a bill that required trans people to use the bathroom that matched the sex listed on their birth certificate had understandably caused outrage. Overnight, it seemed like every right won by and for those who were the most discriminated against and had the least power would be contested.

I took the stage and looked out at the young faces in the audience. I began by offering to stick around afterwards if people needed someone to talk to. Then I talked about the accessibility of photography and how art could be used to change people's perceptions. I shared the stories—the griefs, the traumas, the joys—of some of my subjects, so many of whom had fought back against hate in creative and inspiring ways. By the time I was done, I could sense that the mood had lifted—most of the audience lingered in their seats, eager to continue the conversation.

Although my heart always swells when I'm approached by fierce Muslimahs at events, I was surprised to see that my talk had attracted others who just wanted to be in a place where they felt accepted. A young white lesbian couple stood out among the people of colour. They'd driven hours just for the chance to be with other queer people. One of them, who was in the military, spoke about the homophobia they endured in their small town. Her partner had recently been subjected to conversion therapy at the request of her parents. Their story jolted me with the harsh reminder that one doesn't need to leave North America to witness incidents of cruelty toward queer people. More and more attendees shared their stories and fears—it became clear that people were hungry to spend time in the company of others like them. And so that day, as we had before and surely would again, we began the long process of healing.

North Carolina had cast a spell on me. Although the people I met there were reeling from the election results, their resilience was inspiring and contagious. And their hospitality, even in challenging times, was a revelation. The day after my talk, I took a train from Raleigh to Durham to meet up with Saba and Laila. Saba picked me up at the station looking gorgeous and regal, her head wrapped in a hijab she wore as a turban. Her mannerisms exuded an elegance and refinement that is taught through upbringing. As usual with my subjects, I felt an instant familiarity and kinship with her, as though we were relatives in a past life. When I watched her interact with Laila, the energy was powerful. I could feel the electricity between them, even when they were at opposite ends of the room. Watching Laila and Saba made me understand how loving someone can be a radical act when the world denies you love. Suddenly, I longed to be loved.

Saba is a mixed-media visual artist whose work explores American Muslim identity and challenges Islamophobia. In her small studio, every surface was dusted with glitter, and on one wall hung an illustration of a woman in a hijab holding a banana like a telephone, above her a speech bubble with the words FUCK TRUMP. This was a motif in Saba's work—characters who seemed, to me at least, like hijab-wearing superheroes. I wanted to live in the world she constructed, where Muslim women are aware of their superpowers.

Laila's room was in the back of the house, where she would play the drums to blow off steam after a day of working as an organizer. Gay marriage had been legal in North Carolina for only a very short amount of time. Fearing they would lose their rights as a couple after Trump came into power, Saba and Laila had gone to the Durham courthouse to get married. In photographs from the day, Saba has queerified a kurta by wearing a turban.

Saba had asked her close friends, a community of queer artists of colour, some of whom were Muslim, to organize a welcome party for me. I was incredibly touched by the warm Southern hospitality. The sense of community was infectious. *Inshallah* and *Mashallah* were casually woven into conversations about activism and dating, and into the literature—especially poetry—that was helping everyone cope during these trying times. Many of the party guests were artists who'd moved to Durham for its affordable rent and vibrant community of creative queer people of colour. For some, it was a resting place before they made their way to bigger cities like New York and Miami. We talked about the haunting relevance of Octavia Butler's *Parable of the Sower* in the context of the election, about organizing in times of heightened chaos and preparing for the apocalypse. One Muslim friend talked about crafting signs to protest the KKK, after it was announced that they would be throwing a parade to celebrate Trump's win.

Witnessing politically minded queers in North Carolina, many of whom were also Muslim, was especially revelatory for me, because I often found people back home in Toronto to be apathetic and apolitical, perhaps a result of the comfort and ambivalence that advanced queer rights can breed. Many Canadians who enjoyed the fruits of decades of activism did not see any need to advocate for the rights of queer and trans people of colour. In my experience, progress in many circles had given way to passivity. When I launched my photo project, someone actually asked me if there was even a need for it, because "things are so great in Canada for queers. What's left to fight for?"

Saba's friends were all committed to the idea of fighting for a just world—not just for equal rights for themselves but for others as well. I saw their need to protest and demand justice for African Americans, who were so often unfairly targeted and shot by the police in North Carolina, as an extension of their Muslim faith. In their desire for change and the way it shaped their art, I saw myself reflected back at me. No wonder I felt so at home there.

Although the fear that Islamophobia would escalate under a Trump presidency felt very real, the mood at the party highlighted the group's resilience. They insisted on fighting back, no matter what. Their spirit and courage was so inspiring, and so different from the narrative of victimhood prevalent in mainstream media about Muslim women, that I decided to pitch a new story to *The Guardian* about their feelings in the aftermath of the election, accompanied by a photo essay. I wanted to know how they did it, what their fears were, and what fuelled them. The three people I interviewed and photographed were Saba, Sufia, and Laila.

Saba discussed how, like many people in America, she was balancing a lot of different feelings. There was fear for what the administration was going to do and how it would affect her and the people she loved. "Our safety, our survival, is routinely threatened in the name of some hypothetical greater safety that does not include us," she told me. "What they are trying to keep safe is white supremacy, what they are trying to protect is their own power."

Saba was scared about hate crimes, healthcare, same-sex marriage, reproductive rights, voter suppression, Muslim registries, and deportations. She mentioned how she'd been noticing more and more people showing up to protests. As a result of the election, people had started coming together to hear directly from those affected by racist policies and to speak out in solidarity.

I photographed Sufia on a walk through a gorgeous forest right after a rainfall. The muted colours of the chador around her bare shoulders matched the bark of the oak tree I shot her against. The rich greens and beautiful browns of the fabric and her eyes played harmoniously with the similar shades of the tree. (The trees in Durham are breathtakingly beautiful, with wild and dramatic trunks and an imposing height that makes you pause to acknowledge the history they've soaked in. I've yet to see a tree in Durham that isn't extraordinary.) Sufia told me about how, at this point in her life, her Muslim identity was a political one. Moving to Durham and finding other queer Muslims had had a profound influence on her relationship with Islam. Through building connections to her newfound community, she learned that she no longer had to decide between being queer and being Muslim, that her Muslim identity is inherently queer because she is.

"Islam in its purest form is simply a way of life," she said. "From its teachings, I've gathered a deep appreciation and respect for the concept of inner struggle, and believe that this is the work every human needs to do to be healthy."

As part of her work, Laila went door to door to talk to working-class people of colour about the economic struggles in their community. She was often tasked with trying to identify ways to move people into organizing and taking action. Laila talked about witnessing post-traumatic slave syndrome in a lot of African Americans she spoke with, "a deep numbing and hopelessness from generational trauma" that blacks have in America. As a black queer Muslim, Laila identified with the feeling of hopelessness she recognized in other African Americans she met; she admitted that she experienced it every day. And yet she always managed to tap back into her strength.

"We exist," she told me, "and we're fierce as fuck."

The day the news broke about Trump's Muslim ban, my editor at Public Radio International asked me if I could file a story about it. Protests had broken out at JFK Airport in New York City, as well as at airports in Chicago, San Francisco, and Washington, D.C. Immigrants, including U.S. green-card holders, had been detained as a result of Trump's executive order that placed restrictions on people travelling from several countries with a Muslim-majority population.

I told her I needed some time to think about it. Then I hung up, went to bed, and sobbed for hours. The news reminded me of my Ahmadi family being treated like criminals by religious extremists in Pakistan. Islamophobia is not a new phenomenon, but this time, its cruel reality and its consequences for families, many of whom had escaped a dangerous life in the countries they were from, was a little too close to home. Families separated from one another reminded me of childhood fears I'd buried. Would we always be fighting for a chance to be treated with compassion and dignity?

In the end, I told the editor that this story brought back memories of my own trauma and made me feel powerless, and I didn't feel like reliving that. I'd learned that I was much more interested in the connections that emerge in the aftermath than in the fear, anger, and presumptions that immediately follow a traumatic event affecting Muslims. (An earlier story I had written for this editor, about Americans who'd converted to Islam after 9/11, in an environment of increased Islamophobia, was more about how so many Americans suffered from a lack of spirituality in their lives. I came out of it with a better understanding of human beings and myself.) So, instead of filing a story on the Muslim ban, I made a donation to the ACLU and reached out to my American queer Muslim friends to see how they were feeling and to see if I could provide emotional support.

Whenever my photo project or my writing gets any sort of press, my brother expresses concerns for my safety. He's worried I might get threats from homophobes and Islamophobes. Bilal, now a grown man, is a giant and imposing figure who gets around on a tiny scooter that he's a little too big for. He challenges the sexist and homophobic attitudes of his straight friends every day and dutifully takes my mom to her biweekly spa appointments. "Please let me know if you need me to help you deal with any of that stuff," he offers, although I'm unsure what his protection might look like. (I imagine him, scooter folded under his arm and helmet still on his head, guarding me as I hunch over my laptop feverishly typing up stories about homophobia within Islam.)

To make him feel better, I tell him that I haven't received any threats so far. Which is true. "Do you receive death threats from Muslim militants?" is often the first question I'm asked by the press, eclipsing questions about the stories in my project that challenge the limited narratives that exist when it comes to Muslims. Perhaps because of my experience as an Ahmadi child in Pakistan, fear usually doesn't deter me from working on the project or from writing what I feel I have no choice but to write. I've already experienced what living in fear feels like. Some of my Muslim activist friends also expressed concerns about my writing a memoir. Would writing about my arranged marriage feed into the already prevalent Islamophobic attitudes? What would my parents think about me writing about queer sex and about the sexual abuse I experienced as a child? I don't know the answers to those questions, but

I do know that not being able to talk about those experiences significantly harmed me as I was coming to terms with my queer identity. I don't think fear should dictate how we seek answers, connect, and help each other heal. Growing up, I wish I'd had access to queer Muslim writers and artists who saw, felt, and feared like I did. Who didn't want to denounce Islam and instead wanted to see whether there was still a place for them in it. Who hurt like I did. Perhaps if I had, I would have sought comfort, company, and answers in their work when I was at my loneliest.

That said, I'm also very aware that I haven't photographed queer Muslims in countries where queer rights aren't protected by law. The one exception is Turkey, which is predominantly Muslim. When I photographed my subjects in Istanbul, they asked that I not show their faces because they feared for their safety.

Although I have never returned to Lahore, my project has connected me to queer Muslims in Pakistan, many of whom ask when I will come visit them. But would I feel safe going back to Pakistan as someone who is queer and Ahmadi? Again, I'm not sure. I would love to photograph and interview the inspiring trans community that's mobilizing there and fearlessly engaging with social and political issues, taking up space where they're told they don't have the right to. I long to rediscover the country that birthed me with a pack of queers who tirelessly fight back, who could make me feel that there is a place for me in my hometown. Maybe one day I'll roam the streets of Karachi and Lahore and confirm all the ways my body remembers them.

Recently, Bilal asked me, "Why do you need to call yourself Muslim?" Maybe it's our age difference, but we've never really discussed his relationship with Islam at any great length. I thought about his question. Why do I feel loyalty toward Islam when, as Bilal sees it, Islam isn't always kind toward Muslims like me?

The reality is that this identity has shaped the way I see the world, and the way others see me, in a way that is beyond my control. Being Muslim is one of the only absolutes about myself I can be sure of. It serves as an anchor when I'm lost at sea. It helps me come back to myself, and it leads me to others who've struggled to reconcile seemingly disparate parts of themselves. For me, it's not something I can put on and take off, like a garment. There's no denying that my identity as a queer Muslim is the lens through which I see and engage with so many aspects of my daily life: fashion, music, literature, social media, politics, history, activism, sexuality, gender, faith, art. Basically, everything.

Not everyone is equipped for activism in the traditional sense—marching, writing letters to officials—but dedicating your life to understanding yourself can be its own form of protest, especially when the world tells you that you don't exist. Throughout my childhood, I faced the very real fear that revealing my identity would put me in danger. Once I started figuring out the many factors that defined me, I was able to offer insight from the point of view I'd searched for my entire life. I began to look outside myself; I understood my place in the world, and now I wanted to help others do the same.

Maybe this identity—this label I wear that defines me—is my house. And my voice was in here all along. My siblings have the keys, and my parents are finally regular visitors here. Maybe the roof opens on a hinge, to show that there are no rigid limits, no boundary between this house and the sky, the rest of the world. What luck, to have this house, with its solid foundation, this home that supports me as I refine my perspective, over and over and over again.

Dear Samra,

Being a seven-year-old is hard work. No matter what grown-ups think, it's stressful. Especially for you, someone who likes to know the whys, the whens, the wheres, the hows, and the whos. There's just no certainty these days. Other seven-year-olds might feel fine busying themselves with playing, teasing, and running around, but that's not the life for you. You always want to know the meaning behind everything. "My serious beti" is how your mother introduces you to guests. That will never change. You'll always be quiet and serious, and that's okay. Don't beat yourself up over it. It doesn't mean that you won't also experience an immense amount of joy in your life.

Breathe.

There will be so much joy! Being quiet doesn't mean you don't have anything to say. It's okay to take time to think about how certain things make you feel and to not know right away. You have permission. You'll find times when it'll be right for you to say something. And you will.

Seeking answers is one of the biggest gifts you've been given. But also know that there is so much fun in not knowing and being delighted by what you learn. The joy of discovery is one of the biggest pleasures you'll ever know. It will warm your heart and make you so thrilled to be alive.

Breathe.

You'll get to know many things: how it feels to inspire people and to discover kindness in unexpected places, how the sunrise looks on opposite sides of the world, and how smart and brilliant your siblings are. But most important: yourself. You'll be okay, because your curiosity will lead you to where you need to be. Always listen to that voice in your head and to the people you suspect are smart and can teach you things. Smart people will save you. Love them, get to know them, and ask them what they think.

Breathe.

Like you, your parents will change. Many times. Be kind and forgiving when they do. Although there will be many times in life when you'll feel like you've landed somewhere you're not supposed to be, know that your curiosity and desire for knowledge will pull you back to safety. You'll be okay. Know that.

Love,

Samra

Acknowledgments

There are many people I owe gratitude to for making this book possible. I'd like to thank my editor, David Ross, for his never-ending insight and brilliance. For believing.

I'm grateful for friends who held me close as I unpacked the trauma of the past three decades while writing this book: Sarah, Shima, and Alexa. Thank you for loving me so intuitively. I'd also like to thank Mair Ellis for helping me make sense of it all and for reminding me to breathe.

I'm forever indebted to Abi Slone and Megan Richards for seeing me before I see myself. For inspiring me to dream in the most vibrant colours.

Thanks are due to Marcin Wisniewski for curating my very first queer Muslim photo show, which started it all. Your allyship and tenderness mean the world to me.

I'd also like to thank El-Farouk Khaki for creating a safe space for queer Muslims and for being a pioneer. For your generosity of wisdom and activism and for leading the way. For helping us queer Muslims feel safe in a world that tells us we don't have the right to exist. For being a true advocate for compassion and kindness.

I wouldn't have begun this journey if the queer Muslim subjects I interviewed and photographed didn't trust me to see them. I'm forever grateful to each one of them for sharing their hopes, dreams, fears, and joys with me and for inspiring me to be my authentic self.

If you are a queer Muslim looking for support, Salaam Canada is a wonderful organization dedicated to creating space for people who identify as both queer and Muslim. For a list of support groups for queer Muslims around the world, visit salaamcanada.info.

A NOTE ON THE TYPE

The body of *We Have Always Been Here* has been set in Lyon Text, a typeface designed by Kai Bernau. The roman weight was designed as part of Bernau's degree project at the Royal Academy of Art, but he later went on to expand the typeface and released it with Commercial Type in 2009. Although Lyon Text draws from the renaissance typefaces of Robert Granjon, it has a strong contemporary feel. Notably, at its launch it was adopted as the primary text face for *The New York Times Magazine*. Since then, many other publications have favoured it for its elegance and readability.